# READ BETTER FASTER

# READ

# BETTER

# FASTER

*How to Triple Your Reading Speed and Comprehension Without Speed Reading, Skimming, or Skipping*

# DEBBIE DRUM

Published by TCK Publishing

**www.TCKPublishing.com**

Get discounts and special deals on our best selling books at

**www.tckpublishing.com/bookdeals**

# CONTENTS

# FOREWORD

I AM SO EXCITED to share my new method of reading faster with you—a method that will give you the power to read any book faster with full comprehension. In fact, with my method, I can guarantee you will read at least one book in seven days (you will definitely be able to read more books in that time period, but I will guarantee at least one). Even if the book is over three hundred pages, my guarantee still stands. Does that sound a bit bold and impossible? Well, you're in for a real treat!

If you have trouble reading fast or lose concentration and focus when you read, then you are in the right place to completely change your life. This will open up a whole new world because it will allow you to read and *complete* books faster than you ever imagined. I've tested this method to solve my own problems with reading books excruciatingly slowly. My results? The first week of doing this method, I read four books—three business books and one fiction book. The total number of pages was roughly 950. I was reading about one hour per day and doing this part time, as I worked my business during the day. This was unheard of for me. It used to take me months to get through one business book—if I even finished it at all. I am now reading a *consistent* four to five hundred words per minute with this method. I am going to show you how you can do this, too.

Books, especially big books, used to be impossible for me to get through. I would lose focus and get bored very quickly...even with books I wanted to read. Sadly, I wouldn't get through most of the books I purchased. Ultimately, reading became a daunting task. I eventually got so fed up with my inability to read quickly and easily that I pretty much stopped reading books altogether, except for the occasional short and easy-to-read, self-help book. To advance my career and skillset, I had to figure out how to learn in different ways other than reading books (we'll talk more about alternatives to reading in Chapter 3). I had to accept my "disability" and stop reading books for many years if I wanted to get anywhere fast. It was frustrating, and I knew I was at a huge disadvantage compared to my peers who were reading dozens of books each year.

I always said I would read *Harry Potter* when I turned fifty, when presumably, I would have a bit more time on my hands—at least I think I would, but I am not too sure. Using The BuzzRead Method I am going to show you, I read the first *Harry Potter* book in seven days— while still working full-time, *and* I was also reading another book and had started to write this book! This was a dream come true for me.

To be honest with you, I wasn't even that interested in reading *Harry Potter*; I just wanted to see what all the buzz was about, and, more importantly, I wanted to prove to myself that I could read a large novel in a week. Turned out that wizardry and magic is not really my cup of tea, but I read the book in a week, and if I had tried reading it the traditional way, I would have *never* gotten through it as fast as I did! *Never*! With my disinterest in the topic, I probably wouldn't have gotten past chapter three. Now, when I read a three hundred-page book where I have more interest in the topic, I can speed through the entire book in about three or four days and with near-perfect retention.

By the way, throughout this book, you will hear me refer to the "traditional way" of reading. I am simply talking about regular reading—the good, ol' fashioned, eyes to page—or screen. As you will soon see, my BuzzRead Method is not a "regular" style of reading, so I will just refer to regular reading as traditional. In fact, this method does not one hundred percent apply to folks who only read physical books. The BuzzRead Method is a modern-day strategy, so it relies heavily on electronic books that you read on a Kindle device, smartphone, tablet, desktop, or laptop. However, with that said, I do talk about how The BuzzRead Method helps you learn to read physical books faster. Also, after hearing some feedback from die-hard physical-book fans, I talk about a way you can use the method I am teaching with physical books, as well. I wanted to be up front with you from the beginning, so if you hate electronic books, this method might not be for you. If you love electronic books, then you are in for a real treat!

## THE MEANING BEHIND BUZZREAD

I named my method "The BuzzRead Method" because, well, first, everyone who knows me knows I'm a bee, and I love bees because my name, Deborah, means Bee in Hebrew. Every holiday, my friends get me all bee-related items. From socks to t-shirts, stuffed animals, stickers, dog toys, you name it; I have it. My world is covered in bees. Second, a honey bee's wings stroke incredibly fast—about two hundred beats per second—and that's where the buzzing sound comes from. A honey bee can fly for up to six miles and move as fast as fifteen miles per hour. The name just made sense because after I reveal the method to you, you will be buzzing along and getting through books faster than ever before.

Are you as excited as I am? I hope so! Let's get started.

First, let's talk about what to expect out of this book.

## WHAT TO EXPECT & GUARANTEED RESULTS

Before I outline The BuzzRead Method for you, we're going to cover the foundational skills you'll need to make this method work. You can't and shouldn't jump into this haphazardly. First, if you are a slow reader or you just want to read faster, you are going to understand that it's really not your fault you read slowly, and you are also going to understand the reasons behind why you read slowly in the first place. It's easy for us to come down on ourselves for our weaknesses, but it's time to stop doing that. It stops right now, you hear? Our weaknesses become our strengths when we decide to use our creativity to turn our weakness into a strength. That's what's going to happen for you when you start using The BuzzRead Method.

So, in Chapter 1, you'll learn a little bit about me and my struggles with reading slowly. I only share this with you so you'll understand my hardships, which you will probably relate to, even if your reading skills are already good.

Next, in Chapter 2, you'll discover and understand the best way *you* learn. The three ways are listed below. We don't all learn the same way, and we are all unique. People learn in three different ways—and some of us are extra special, requiring a combination of these learning methods to get optimal results.

1. Visual
2. Auditory
3. Kinesthetic

If you are a slow reader like I am, you might be an audio, video/visual learner. You might need to see something *and* hear something for it to really sink in to your brain. That's perfectly fine. Knowing the way you learn best will give you an advantage from here on out because you will be able to optimize the way you learn, so you can learn faster and with less effort.

In Chapter 3, we'll talk about other specific ways to learn, such as listening and watching videos, and why these ways of learning are more effective for many.

In Chapter 4, we'll talk about some reasons people read slowly and the bad habits people have that cause the books they read to seem never ending.

Next, in Chapter 5, we will talk about whether speed-reading courses and speed-reading apps actually work to help you read faster. I've tried both expensive courses and apps, so I'll share with you some insight about my experience and how you can decide if these tools are right for you.

In Chapter 6, it's finally time to reveal The BuzzRead Method to you because you will be ready to hear it. As much as you probably want to, please don't jump ahead because each chapter builds on the next, and you need to be able to see the entire picture to get optimal results. It's a small amount of time to dedicate to achieving success for the rest of your life.

We'll then talk about why this method is different than any you've seen or heard before.

Before we move on to actually setting up to use this method, in Chapter 8 we'll dive into some memory techniques. Now, you might be wondering why we are talking about memory in a book that shows you how to read faster. The answer is simple. Because you will be reading more, you need a way to remember the information you are ingesting. The last thing you want to do is read more and not remember a blessed thing. I am going to show you ways to retain all the new information you'll be acquiring as a result of reading more.

I will show you how to retain far more of the information you read, so you never again forget the ideas and stories you need to succeed. It's one thing to read fast, but it's another thing if the content is actually sticking, as opposed to going in one ear and then right out the other. This is a big part of the process. I definitely don't want to teach you this amazing new superpower and then have you forgetting the information as fast as you are ingesting it. After all, the purpose of reading is to learn and remember important information and good stories, right? And that's exactly what you'll be able to do once you start implementing this system for reading more and remembering more of wat you read. We need to create systems, visualizations, and stories in our brain, so we remember the content. I am going to show you a few techniques to use, so you can ensure you are not going to forget what you read...especially if you *have* to remember the content—for a test, for instance, or to make more money, etc.

In chapters 9-13, I will show you how to set up the technical aspects of The BuzzRead Method and how to get it to work for you. You can work the method on a mobile device, a tablet device, and even on a desktop or laptop. It's not hard to set up, and I give you step-by-step instructions you can easily follow.

We will not cover a great deal of detail on speed-reading techniques in this book, but I do have some ideas and advice for you in chapter 14. As you will see, my method is a modern-day method, and as far as I know, I'm the first to cover this material in a book. So if you want speed-reading techniques, there are tons of books and courses out there by speed-reading experts. In fact, I recommend you check them out because it's always good to have those skills, too. What you will find, however, is that The BuzzRead Method will ultimately enhance your overall reading skills and will open the door for other speed-reading techniques—that's why I love this method.

While The BuzzRead Method will change your life in a very positive way, in Chapter 15, we will talk about some pitfalls and traps to avoid with your new superpower. As with any system, there are pluses and minuses, so I will be sure to let you see the full picture. The BuzzRead Method will help you go through content fast, but this can come with traps, and we'll cover those, so you don't fall into them.

We'll end by talking about how to practice the method and make more improvements to your reading. We'll talk about how to measure your success and create reading goals. I know I am going to create a reading monster out of you, so I'll show you all the advantages that come along with your new and amazing skill. I will even show you how to gain financial freedom from your new skill.

## THE ULTIMATE OUTCOME

The formation of any habit comes from constant practice, and when you practice The BuzzRead Method, you will reap the tremendous benefits that come with it.

Here are five main benefits you'll get out of practicing The BuzzRead Method.

1. **Read More Books**: Are you a student, studying for a test? Are you a mom-to-be who needs to read several books on caring for your newborn? Are you an entrepreneur, looking to skyrocket your career? Being able to read more books will be an extreme advantage for you!

2. **Eliminate Sub-Vocalization:** One of the reasons people read slowly is because they sub-vocalize. Sub-vocalization is speaking each word in your head while you read. Most of us were taught to sub-vocalize when reading, and this creates the habit of only comprehending what you read when the words are heard in your head. You see, fast readers don't read every single word. Their eyes skim, and they recognize words automatically like you do with street signs or brand names. If you sub-vocalize, that will begin to stop and eventually, with enough practice, completely go away. The BuzzRead Method will allow you to move smoothly through the lines on the page or screen, and you will find you are sub-vocalizing less and less, until you reach the point when you don't do it anymore at all.

3. **Strengthen Your Eye Muscles:** Another reason people read slowly is because they haven't properly trained their eye muscles to read efficiently and effectively. Your eyes need training in order to read quickly, just like your pecs need training if you want to bench press two hundred pounds. You don't get strong muscles without working out, and you don't read fast without giving your eyes the workout they need to perform at an optimal level. Practicing The BuzzRead Method will give your eyes the workout, so you can read for a longer amount of time without tiring.

4. **Retain and Comprehend More:** As you will see, with The BuzzRead Method you will be reading every single word, and you won't be skimming as if you were speed-reading. If you aren't skipping, this means you will read and retain important information you might have missed if you were using speed-reading techniques.

5. **Become Smarter and More Knowledgeable:** Who doesn't want this? This is the reason we read in the first place. Being able to consume more in a shorter amount of time will only make you smarter.

Here's one last bonus benefit...

6. **Enjoy Reading More:** Getting through reading material faster will allow you to start enjoying reading, rather than being frustrated because you are going through the material slowly or tiring quickly. I was ecstatic when I was able to read the first *Harry Potter* book in only seven days and finish life-changing business books faster than I could have ever dreamed!

With that said, let's get started...

# CHAPTER 1

# IS THIS YOU, TOO?

I AM A REALLY slow reader. I have always been a slow reader. The average reader reads two hundred words per minute; I used to barely be able to read one hundred words per minute. I was never taught the right skills from an early age on how to read fast.

I always envied people who said they can read a book in a couple hours or an afternoon. That was never the case for me. I couldn't even read thirty pages in an afternoon, let alone a whole book.

Before I developed the method I am going to share with you in this book, this was my story...

For as long as I can remember, when I read, I read every single word in my mind—known as sub-vocalization, as explained above—which you are not supposed to do for effective, fast reading. I also lost focus easily, and my mind would start to wander. I couldn't concentrate and read at the same time. The daunting task of trying to read an entire book exhausted me. I wanted to get through the material fast, but for some reason, I just couldn't. I never struggled with concentration before, so the issue of not being able to focus when I read was odd for me.

Do you remember the SATs and those long, boring passages you had to read and answer detailed questions about? That was torture! Reading long passages that bore no relevance to real life and having to answer specific and tricky, detailed questions was too much for my reading skills at the time. I took study courses and studied for months but still performed well below my expectations on standardized tests that involved reading comprehension. Even though I was always a slow reader, I still managed to have a 3.9 average in my first year of college at SUNY Cortland in upstate NY. I transferred out after freshman year to SUNY Binghamton, just forty minutes south. I got accepted into the School of Management Program and managed to keep a steady 3.5 average throughout the next three years. I dealt with my inability to read quickly by simply working harder and studying more. I did everything a bit slower than my peers, all of whom seemed to be able to read faster than I could. At times, reading slowly may have even been an advantage for me because it forced me to pay more attention to small details other students would often overlook. When I finally developed The BuzzRead Method, I wanted to make sure that attention to detail and memorization would not be sacrificed simply for the sake of reading faster.

In 2010, I started a business, and I soon realized I could learn a lot quicker by listening to content instead of reading. When I listened to podcasts, videos, and audiobooks, I was able to get through material a lot faster, and I was also retaining much more information. I was able to listen to audio everywhere with my iPhone—at the gym, commuting on the train, and even walking my dogs. This opened up a whole new world for me. I was finally on a level playing field...almost.

Even though I was learning a lot by listening to audio programs, I knew I was still missing out. While listening to audio helped me overcome my reading disadvantage to some extent, it just wasn't the same as reading books. I wanted to read books that friends, colleagues, gurus, and even Oprah recommended to me. What a waste. All the great books I really wanted to read ended up collecting dust, first on my nightstand and then, eventually, on the bookshelf.

This sad story does turn around...

Modern technology now makes it possible for slow readers like me, and maybe even you, to read any book from beginning to end quickly and to retain the information. I am going to show you how to do just that.

The very first week, The BuzzRead Method allowed me to read four books in a week and eleven books—yes, even big books—in thirty days!

I know this is going to help you because it helped me. I also know this will help young people, too, if they show signs of slow reading and lack of retaining information when they read. This method just plain works.

The beautiful thing about this is the technology that will allow you to essentially speed-read is free. The technology does all the hard work for you, and I'll show you how easy it can be to get started right away, without spending a dime.

But first, the fact is, we need to explore the different ways people learn.

CHAPTER 2

# PEOPLE LEARN IN DIFFERENT WAYS—IT'S NOT YOUR FAULT

IF YOU READ SLOWLY, it's not your fault.

Every single person on the face of this planet has a fingerprint unlike anyone else's. Even identical twins. That's just one of the many things that makes us each unique and special in our own way. Another thing that sets us apart as individuals is our unique learning style.

I've been trained by top sales professionals, and one of the things we focused on is how people learn. Often, the way you learn is similar to the way you speak. You can usually tell how a person learns just by listening to the words they say. When you start to pay attention to the specific words people use to describe their experiences in life, you'll be amazed at how much more quickly you can get to know someone.

There are as many unique learning styles as there are individuals; however, most learning styles tend to fall under one of three different categories, namely auditory, visual, or kinesthetic.

While the majority of people gain knowledge through a combination of all three learning styles, knowing and taking advantage of the primary learning style that comes naturally to you—and to others if you are teaching someone else—is essential for enhancing and enjoying the educational experience as much as possible.

To take this one step further, if you are in the business of sales, knowing someone's learning style is money in the bank. The ability to quickly pick up on how someone learns will allow you to communicate in a manner they truly understand, and your connection will be stronger, which usually leads to a positive outcome such as building rapport and, eventually, making the sale. The opposite is true, too. For example, if someone is an auditory learner and you're showing them charts, graphs, and statistics, you might lose the person's interest and lose the sale while you're at it. This is why matching the style of the other person is very important, and the sooner you can master this skill, the quicker you'll become more successful at connecting with others.

## How to Identify Your Primary Learning Style

How do you correctly identify which one of the three major learnings styles you tend to lean toward naturally?

There are several common factors that are noticeable in people who share each primary learning style:

### Auditory

Auditory learners do best when they are able to absorb and comprehend information by listening. They understand, remember, and are more receptive to information they hear.

If you're an auditory learner, hearing information and speaking during the learning process is essential if you want to learn and retain more information more quickly and easily.

Do you often find yourself doing any of the following things?

- Reading out loud.
- Moving your lips while reading silently.
- Preferring to discuss information and ideas with others.

If so, you are likely an auditory learner and will benefit the most from teaching styles that include being able to hear and listen to the information shared.

Auditory learners will often use words and language that utilize sound words such as: "I hear what you are saying," "clear as a bell," "lend me your ear," "pay attention to," "does that sound right?"

Listen for sound words such as:

| | |
|---|---|
| Hear | Sound |
| Clear | Listen |

When you hear someone using several words, phrases, or metaphors that relate to hearing, it's likely they are an auditory learner.

## Visual

Visual learners remember and are more receptive to information they can see. However, unlike auditory learners, this primary learning group is often divided into two major subgroups:

**Linguistic**—People who are visual linguistic learners do best when they can absorb and comprehend information through reading and writing. They tend to remember things they see written down and pay better attention to interactions they can watch.

**Spatial**—Unlike their counterparts, individuals who are visual spatial learners do not do well with the written word. Instead, they learn best by using diagrams, charts, illustrations, videos, and other similar visual tools.

If you want to know if you learn primarily through the visual style, look for clues in the following habits:

- Visualizing what you learn in your mind.
- Remembering things once you write them down.
- Using colors and pictures to enhance the learning experience.

Visual learners tend to use language such as: "I see what you mean," "I get the picture," "What's your view?"

Listen for visual words such as:

| | |
|---|---|
| See | View |
| Look | Picture |
| Clear | |

### Kinesthetic

Kinesthetic learners retain and receive information that involves elements of touch and movement. Like visual learners, this primary learning group can be further divided into two subgroups:

**Kinesthetic**—People who need to move and "do" something in order to stay focused are kinesthetic learners. They do best when the learning experience involves some kind of physical activity.

**Tactile**—While the need for external stimulation is equally as strong in tactile learners, these individuals learn primarily through their sense of touch and using their hands to perform tasks.

If you find yourself doing the following things, you are most likely a kinesthetic learner:

- Using highlighters or tracing lines with your fingers while reading.
- Moving your hands while talking.
- Needing to take regular breaks while doing a task.

Kinesthetic learners tend to use language like: "that feels right," "How does that grab you?" "Let me try."

Listen for physical words like:

| | |
|---|---|
| Get a hold of or get a handle on | Feel |
| Grab | Try |
| Grasp | |

## FIND THE LEARNING STYLE THAT WORKS BEST FOR YOU

As you can see, all three learning styles are somewhat connected. Ideally, you need all three to learn, but there is always one dominant learning style that is present. I learn best by listening to content.

You need to find the style that works for you. I am guessing the visual style is not your strong suit if you are reading this book in the first place. If you are reading this book merely to learn this method, well, then all of this is still important to know.

These days, because there are many different opportunities to learn in different ways—now more than ever, and it will just keep on getting better—you should not be ashamed if you are not strong in learning a particular way, and you have to learn, adapt, and grow with the way that works best for you.

Take advantage of what makes you stronger, and you will rise to the next level. It wasn't easy admitting to the world that I am a slow reader. This truth doesn't make me dumb, and I feel empowered and lucky that we live in an age where there is technology available to give us what we need to grow and become more knowledgeable.

If you are a slow reader, in the next chapter, I'll show you how audio and video could be the answer for you.

| Review |
| --- |
| There are 3 different types of learners: auditory, visual, and kinesthetic. |
| Auditory learners learn and retain information quickly and easily by listening; they read out loud and prefer to discuss information and ideas with others. |
| Visual learners learn and retain information quickly and easily by seeing; they are either Linguistic (they learn best by reading and writing) or Spatial (they learn best by using charts, illustrations, etc.) |
| Kinesthetic learners learn best when the elements of touch and movement are involved; they are either Kinesthetic (they require physical activity) or Tactile (they learn primarily through their sense of touch). |
| See if you can pinpoint which learning style you identify with. Remember, this could be a combination of a few, but there should be one dominant trait you can relate to. |

CHAPTER 3

# WHY LISTENING AND WATCHING MAKES LEARNING EASIER

IN 2010, I BEGAN to realize the power of learning with video. By then, the internet was booming, and online video was becoming very popular. It wasn't all cat videos and karaoke cover songs—there were also educational and informational videos on almost every topic under the sun. Today, as you can imagine, online video has evolved even more, and you can learn just about anything by going to **http://youtube.com** and typing in your question. There's a good chance you will find the answer you are looking for from several different videos. People are putting a lot of time and money into video production, now more than ever.

So what does this mean for learning?

Have you ever seen those videos that have talking in the background with moving pictures and drawings throughout? I am sure you have.

Here's an example: **http://debbiedrum.com/talktoanyone**

Essentially, there's a narrator in the background, and the video is showing pictures and drawings of the content the narrator is speaking about. These kinds of videos take a lot of skill and time to make, but for viewers, they can be much more entertaining and memorable than a video of someone who is just standing in front of a camera and speaking.

Have you ever wanted to learn about the importance of bees, and what's going on with bees dying off and why that is so horrible for the world? Then watch this video, and you'll be in the know in only three minutes and twenty-eight seconds. See it here: **http://debbiedrum.com/beesdie**

The reason these videos are easy to watch, understand, interpret, and recall is because they are engaging. Videos like this are very popular and widely successful.

For the same reason, most people find it quite easy to sit through their favorite TV show without their mind wandering and losing concentration.

I am a slow reader, but if you get me on a great fiction book or a topic I really enjoy, I will read that much faster, and my mind won't wander.

When you're fully engaged with a book or a video, you'll stay focused and remember more. Your mind won't wander as it does when you're bored or distracted.

When something is engaging, it's hard not to pay attention to it. In these videos, when you watch the pictures being drawn, a memorable story is being created in your head. This is precisely how our brain remembers information, which we will get to in a bit because visualization is one of the key components of The BuzzRead Method.

If we don't visualize the content and make a story in our brain while we are reading, well, the material is not going to stick, and we won't remember it. Plain and simple. If we are not actively engaged, the information is going to fly out very quickly. This is a huge waste of time.

If you want to learn something quickly to impress your friends at a dinner party—such as what terrible things will happen if the population of bees becomes reduced—then find one of these videos on YouTube. This visual medium allows you to learn about just about any topic in a very short period of time.

Most likely, the main points of the video will stick with you because you will be engaged in the information while you are watching the video.

These kinds of Explainer videos are everywhere! People make them because they work. How do video makers know these videos work? Because their analytics show whether people are watching the videos all the way through—and they *are*! The data shows that people *love* them! Now, imagine you had to read a three hundred-page book on the importance of bees for the Earth. Snoozefest for most of us, right?

Let's dive a bit deeper into the reasons some people read slowly.

| Action Steps |
|---|
| Google search for an article about "What Happens if the Bees Die," or any topic you are interested in learning, and take a few minutes to read it. |
| Then go to http://youtube.com, and watch a short video on the topic. |
| Compare your experiences. Identify which of the two methods was effective in making you retain the information easily and quickly. |

# CHAPTER 4

# WHY DO SOME PEOPLE READ SLOWLY?

IT'S WELL-NOTED that some of the most wealthy and successful people in the world attribute much of their good fortune to the fact that during their lives, they developed a dedicated reading habit.

For some of these avid booklovers, reading up to a thousand pages a day is as easy and natural as making a morning cup of coffee. It's simply part of their daily routine. But make no mistake; consuming that amount of written knowledge everyday requires a voracious appetite for knowledge and the ability to read quickly.

If you are a slow reader, the thought of conquering a new book each week or even one book every month can feel like trying to climb Mount Everest.

So if you do read slowly, why is this so?

Once the probability of a vision problem is safely eliminated, the answer could lie in one or more of a few common reasons:

## LEVEL OF ENGAGEMENT

Have you ever settled down to watch a movie and found yourself fast asleep less than halfway through? That movie probably never got you excited enough to sit all the way through to a nail-biting finish. It could have been that the movie was too boring for you. Or maybe you were too tired or distracted by something else.

The same thing can happen when you're reading a book.

When your level of engagement is low, reading speed and comprehension plummets. On the other hand, when your engagement levels are high, you'll be able to read and comprehend the subject matter much more easily.

If you really want to improve your reading speed, it's best to start with books about topics you actually enjoy because you'll automatically be more engaged when reading something you care about.

However, you should also be able to quickly read material you are not always passionate about. That's part of life. We go through school having to learn different topics, and most of the time it's not always a ball of laughs and entertainment. That is why it's important to be able to consume any type of information, not just information we enjoy.

## CONTENT COMPLEXITY

It stands to reason that it is much easier to read a book quickly if you understand and are comfortable with the author's word choices.

Imagine giving a medical journal to a carpenter or a legal brief to a nurse. Reading content that is far more complex or that contains a lot of unfamiliar words and terms is bound to slow down even the best reader.

This is an often-overlooked factor involved in less-than-optimal reading speeds.

## READING ANXIETY

The truth is that worrying about the fact that you're a slow reader can actually make your problem of being a slow reader even worse. If you're thinking about anything other than the text you're reading, you won't be able to read quickly and remember everything.

By focusing on how slowly you read and constantly thinking about how many pages you have to go to complete your current reading goal, you create an environment that leads to reading anxiety, which can become absolutely crippling.

Part of learning how to read as quickly as you can requires letting go of any thoughts that lead to an uptick in your anxiety levels. Instead of focusing on how fast you're reading, put all your effort into focusing on the content you're reading.

## NOT BEING TAUGHT EARLY ON HOW TO READ PROPERLY

While all the reasons above are completely true, I believe, for me—and this is probably true for others—that we weren't taught the proper way to read at a young, impressionable age. I have a vivid memory of when I was taught to read. The early books were fun to read, and I remember reading them aloud to my mom at the kitchen table while she did the dishes. I was reading slowly, out loud, and every single word. This poor habit transferred to when I read to myself. The only difference was that I wasn't reading aloud.

When you are taught something right from an early age, that's pure gold. Such as when kids are taught a second language when they are young, they learn it much faster than an adult who's trying to learn a second language. It's just easier when you are a kid or a young person to learn a skill that will stay with you and improve the rest of your life. Think about someone in your life who started a skill or a practice early in their life and where they are now because of it. Perhaps you have experienced this for yourself.

More complex reasons for slow reading speeds include factors such as sub-vocalization while reading, reading words one at a time instead of grouping them, regressive reading—having to go back and re-read because you've zoned out—and, believe it or not, having a poor attitude toward the activity of reading itself.

To successfully tackle and overcome the issue of reading slowly, it's important to remember that slow readers—including you—are just as intelligent and capable as anyone else.

If you want to read faster, there are ways you can re-teach yourself how to read, and break bad reading habits. There are speed-reading courses, books, as well as some speed-reading apps.

Let's talk about speed-reading training because if you've been struggling to teach yourself to read faster, then you've probably tried some or all of the following solutions.

| Recap |
| --- |
| Here are four reasons why some people are slow readers: Level of Engagement, Content Complexity, Reading Anxiety, and Not Being Taught Early on How to Read Properly. |
| Level of Engagement: You do not enjoy the book you are reading, or the topic is boring you. |
| Content Complexity: You read content that contain a lot of terms you have never heard before |
| Reading Anxiety: You are focusing too much on your inability to read books fast and are worrying about the number of pages you have to read. |
| Not Being Taught Early on How to Read Properly: Reading word-per-word, regressive reading, having a poor attitude towards reading. |

# CHAPTER 5

# DOES SPEED-READING TRAINING WORK?

FIRST, LET'S DEFINE THE term speed-reading.

Wikipedia says:

> *Speed-reading is any of several techniques used to improve one's ability to read quickly. Speed-reading methods include chunking and minimizing sub-vocalization.*

There are different techniques you can adopt in your reading to avoid having to read every single word of a piece of content or book. Speed-reading is not the ability to read every word really fast.

I got excited when I came across Jim Kwik's "Kwik Reading" course on speed-reading in 2016. I learned about Jim from Lewis Howes' The School of Greatness podcast. Jim Kwik's story resonated with me because he, too, had trouble getting through entire books. When he learned and developed the techniques he now teaches, it worked for him...really well. I went through Jim's material and practiced the techniques but will admit I didn't give it the full practice it needed for me to read faster. Like anything, if you don't put in the time, you don't get the desired outcome! I definitely put some practice in; however, I'll admit, I didn't devote enough to get the job done and engrain the new habits. Turned out, I wasn't patient enough with the system—and yes, I am working on that.

Like many of us in our "microwave society," I wanted results very quickly, and I was often left defeated because I still was not comprehending information when I was practicing. Even while implementing the techniques, I was still up to my old habit of wanting to read every word, and when I wasn't reading every word, the content was just not sticking. The experience was quite frustrating.

Learning how to speed-read does work, but, like anything, there are muscles to develop and new habits to form, and if you don't put in the work to develop the new skills, you won't succeed.

I, on the other hand, was more interested in Jim Kwik's memory techniques that have helped me to memorize talking points better, so I don't have to use notes, and this has also helped me to never forget a name after I hear it (more on that later). I put energy into developing new memory skills that I am still using and benefiting from to this day. I highly recommend all of Jim Kwik's trainings. By the way, I have no affiliation with Jim Kwik; I am just a fan of his work.

Modern technology is a beautiful thing because now there are apps that can help you read faster. Apps and technology do not provide a "quick fix." You still need to put in the time to make them work for you. This means practicing the drills every day, and sometimes several times a day, until your new skills/habits become automatic.

The speed-reading app I like and recommend is called Acceleread.

The app has tons of drills designed to improve your reading speed, ability, and comprehension. It's really great, but again, you have to devote the time to get the results! Dedication and hard work are the two requirements for success.

So, do speed-reading courses and apps work? They do if you put in the time, work, and practice. Using them requires a lot of dedication because you have to unlearn bad habits and form new, helpful ones. Anytime you do that, it's going to take you more than a day to master and retrain your brain.

I desperately needed another way that worked for my learning style. I didn't find one until a lightbulb went off in my head one day...and the method I found completely changed my life!

When I discovered The BuzzRead Method, it opened up my world because now I was able to read books faster than ever! I no longer feel defeated when someone recommends a book to me that I always knew in the back of my mind I would never read because I had a hundred other books in my reading queue! Now, there are no more roadblocks. No more limitations. I no longer feel overwhelmed.

I wish I had discovered this method years ago. The technology has been around for a while, but everything happens for a reason, so the time is now for me to share my discovery with the world!

## UPDATE

While writing this book, I studied the top resources and research on reading and speed-reading. I read several books on the topic—using The BuzzRead Method, of course.

The update I want to share is that I started using some of the speed-reading techniques (more on this later), and my traditional reading style is improving every day. As you will see, The BuzzRead Method will help develop skills to read faster overall, and that is why you can incorporate age-old, speed-reading techniques with this more modern method. Once you get good at reading fast, you can start incorporating techniques to improve your reading even more.

So, let's get into The BuzzRead Method because I know you are probably on the edge of your seats, wanting to know what it's all about!

# CHAPTER 6

# THE BUZZREAD METHOD REVEALED

THE BUZZREAD METHOD MAINLY works with electronic books. As I said earlier, it's a modern-day method of getting through books fast with no problem. In the upcoming sections, I will tell you how it works, then I will tell you why it works and then show you how to set it up.

The BuzzRead Method uses your phone, tablet, or certain e-readers' accessibility function called Text To Speech or TTS. The accessibility function reads text to you with a voice that sounds like a robot. Most popular smartphones and tablets (like iPhones, Samsungs, iPads, and Kindle Fires) have the accessibility function that makes this method free because it's already built into the device and can be activated at any time.

You can download any book (from Kindle or elsewhere), or PDF (which we'll discuss later) and use this method right away. You don't have to purchase an audio version of the book because the TTS will always be waiting for you. There are no additional costs or anything to set up—you just jump into the book.

The great part about this is that you can have your device read text to you as slow or as fast as it's humanly possible to understand. With the device reading the text back to you, it almost forces you to keep engaged, and it forces you to push through parts of books that might be boring or tough to get past.

Before you think—*that's it? The device reads text back to me? Wow, that's great, Debbie*—there is a bit more to the process, and to get all the benefits—and there are a ton of them—*you've got to be actively involved in the process*, and I'll show you how.

There is one absolute mandatory part of The BuzzRead Method that will bring your reading to the next level...fast. Let's discuss.

## MANDATORY PART OF THE PROCESS

Part of the process of using The BuzzRead Method is that you need to follow along with the words as the device reads the text to you. This method isn't like listening to an audiobook; you don't just listen while you walk on the treadmill. We will go into this more in the next chapter.

When I say follow along, I mean skimming or scanning the text. Skimming has somewhat of a different meaning when you use it without The BuzzRead Method, and we will talk more about skimming later. For now, with The BuzzRead Method, your eyes should follow the text as it's being read aloud. This action has a ton of major benefits that will help you with reading fast, comprehending, and retaining more.

**Skimming/Following along is essential to the process for a couple of reasons.**

First, part of learning to read faster in general is developing the muscles in your eyes, so they don't tire easily. If you download any speed-reading app, you will find many of the exercises involve moving your eyes and bouncing your eyes back and forth, down and up, and vertically because as with anything else that requires use of your body, you need to develop the muscles and the muscle memory. Doing these eye exercises will help you to read faster. The exercises are also designed to develop other speed-reading techniques—like chunking— but they also work your eyes to make them stronger.

So the process of you skimming the words and essentially reading along, will help you to read faster when you are reading normally and not relying on a device to read to you.

The second reason skimming is important is this will help with retention, or retaining and remembering the content you read. As mentioned earlier, if you are not actively engaged when you are "reading," if you are just listening and not following along, your mind might wander, and you might lose track of the text. If this happens, you will be in the exact position you were in before you started The BuzzRead Method—reading information that never becomes embedded into your brain. As I alluded to earlier, not comprehending what you've just read is a huge problem for slow readers. Amazing how we can read entire pages of a book and have no clue what we have just read. It's pretty fascinating at the same time. Have you ever zoned out while you were driving but still managed to get to your destination in one piece? The two situations are very similar!

We want to avoid zoning out, and your goal is to be active during the reading process. This is why The BuzzRead Method is different from any other type of speed-reading or listening to an audiobook.

The great part about this method is you can dedicate very little time— as little as thirty minutes a day—and get more done in less time and retain more. This method is unlike traditional reading, where you might only get through twenty pages in thirty minutes if you are lucky, and you still have a long way to go to get through the entire book.

One last benefit of skimming along with the TTS is this helps plant a mental picture in your brain. When you think back to the text later, you will almost be able to see the words on the page in your head, and picture where the text was on the page, what the page looked like and even how the text looked on the page—what was in bold, bullets, italics, etc. It's almost like having a mental photograph of the words on the page. This helps with retention in a major way.

Let's discuss how this is different from listening to an audiobook, which is probably something you are wondering...

| Review |
| --- |
| The BuzzRead Method uses the text-to-speech function on your smartphone, tablet, and certain e-readers. |
| The essential part of the method is skimming along with the text as the phone reads to you. This will improve your overall reading skills, and it will also help with retention. |
| Skimming will help you stay engaged with the content, which is also essential for retention. |

# CHAPTER 7

# HOW THE BUZZREAD METHOD IS *NOT* SIMILAR TO LISTENING TO AUDIOBOOKS...AT ALL

BEFORE I GET TO showing you how to implement The BuzzRead Method, let's talk about why this is not like simply listening to the audio version of a book.

Using the traditional way of reading, I've struggled with getting through books quickly my entire life. Believe me, I've tried audiobooks. I like audiobooks, but I have found there are three major problems with using this method.

First, they are not cheap. Audiobooks, especially for popular books, can cost you upward of twenty dollars each! If you want to read a ton of books, then you better set up a savings account or have a monthly budget for this hobby. If you are reading business books for work, you could write this off as an educational expense (you'll want to speak to an accountant about this first), but even then, it will be an investment. There are audiobook clubs you can join to help bring down the cost per book, but those charge a monthly membership fee, and there are still more disadvantages to relying solely on audiobooks...

The second disadvantage is that not all books are available in audiobook format. Many of the books I really want to listen to are not available on Audible. Limiting yourself to only the books available in audiobook format is not a good plan.

Lastly and most importantly, listening to an audiobook doesn't allow you to become actively engaged in the reading process. You cannot follow along with the text as you do with The BuzzRead Method. Therefore, you run the risk of your mind wandering, becoming distracted, and possibly missing crucial details of what you are reading.

While multi-tasking is a controversial topic, most will argue we can't do two things at once effectively. If you are listening to an audiobook and also paying for your groceries, chances are you will miss crucial parts of the book. If your mind is not actively engaged and envisioning what the book is talking about, it's going to be harder for you to retain the information, and the content will be going in one ear and out the other.

Another minor disadvantage is not liking the narrator. It's not a huge deal, but that matters to some people.

Don't get me wrong, audiobooks are a great innovation and a wonderful way to read. They also come in handy when you have to commute for work or you want to listen to something while you walk the dogs or work out. Audiobooks are great, but if you are trying to improve your reading skills so you don't always have to rely on audio versions of everything you want to read, then you'll want to try The BuzzRead Method.

With audiobooks, I have had to go back to re-listen to certain sections of the book later on because I had forgotten so many details. Why does this happen?

Because your brain works in a certain way when it comes to how you retain information. Read on to learn more.

# CHAPTER 8

# TRAINING YOUR BRAIN
# TO REMEMBER MORE

REMEMBERING AND RETAINING INFORMATION is an important part of your reading journey. It has to be; otherwise, what's the point?

Your brain is the most powerful computer in the world.

Even if you aren't aware of the processes as they happen, your brain is always busy receiving signals and sending signals to every part of your body. You breathe, blink, and can even perform relatively complicated tasks, like driving, without really thinking about it because your brain is just that awesome.

This fact makes it even harder to understand why it's so difficult to remember things at times. For instance, why do we misplace keys, forget anniversaries and birthdays, and even completely space out in the middle of an important presentation?

Here's the secret discovered by leading neuroscientists...

The human brain remembers things most efficiently by forming mental pictures and by making associations. Once you learn how to program your "computer" (brain) correctly with the relevant input, producing the right output is automatic, and being able to access or remember things becomes practically effortless.

Here's how it works...

## How Pictures and Associations Help You Master Memory

Now that you know the basics of how memory works and the kinds of input your brain needs to produce the desired "output" or memory, let's perform a short experiment to see this system in action.

*Try to remember what you had for dinner last Friday night.*

If you were able to clearly and immediately "see" the plate of food you had sitting in front of you, you've successfully used a mental picture to recall the meal and remember exactly what you had.

If it took a bit longer for you to remember, you likely started thinking about what you were doing around dinner time that night.

Perhaps you were ordering pizza because you couldn't bother to cook, and that's what your kids wanted, or you were on a date at a nice Italian restaurant. Maybe you invited a few friends over to join you for some of your famous fish tacos. Maybe you went away for the weekend, and you ate at a fancy restaurant.

If one of these scenarios caused you to create a mental picture of what you had for dinner, you've successfully used an association to trigger the memory.

Pretty cool, right?

Once you completely understand and put the power of pictures and associations into practice, being able to remember just about anything becomes as easy and reliable as using a calculator and trusting that the results you get are consistent and accurate.

## How to Enhance Your Life with Pictures and Associations

Even if you have what you consider to be one of the worst memories in the world, you can learn how to use pictures and associations to successfully boost your recollection powers dramatically.

When people think or say they are horrible with names, well, that just means they don't put any effort into the remembering process. They don't actually listen or even try to remember the name when they hear it. Not because they don't care but because when you are introduced to someone, a few things are going on:

- It's usually something that happens quickly
- The normal process is to introduce yourself back
- Sometimes, you are being introduced to many people at once, which could be overwhelming

So, if one doesn't take the time to actually remember someone's name, it's going to fly in one ear and out the other. If no effort is made, it's not going to just stick in your brain like magic. And that's when people say, "I am horrible with names."

But here's a little trick...

Let's pretend someone says, "Hi, my name is Jennifer." (And maybe Jennifer is a dancer).

You shake Jennifer's hand, and repeat her name. "Hi, Jennifer."

Then you make a mental picture in your mind. You know Jennifer likes dancing, so you can instantly associate Jennifer with Jennifer Grey from *Dirty Dancing*. I just picked that example out of thin air, and it will likely resonate with women because of the *Dirty Dancing* reference, but this method will always work. Take a second to say the name out loud, and then associate the name with someone you know or are familiar with, such as a celebrity with the same name.

If it's not a common name, then ask for the spelling of the name or ask what the meaning of the name is. Then quickly think of a way to recall that person's unique name.

You see how we are taking extra steps to remember the name? It's not as if some people have this magic, super-human power that allows them to always remember names when they meet someone. No. They are using their own memory "formula" to remember what the person's name is. They are able to quickly access the name because they did the work to store it properly. So, again, if you or anyone else says, "I am horrible with names," you know this is completely impossible, and you just need to add effort to the recollection process.

Now, that's just names. You can use systems that have been created to remember just about anything. A presentation, capitals of states, US Presidents, *anything*!

If you have to remember something like for a test or a presentation, you can utilize one or any combination of the following proven, memory-enhancing techniques and systems:

- Peg
- Link
- Keyword
- Loci (Journey)
- Face-Name
- Phonetic-Number

Each one of these systems focuses on creating mental images and associations that rapidly improve your ability to retain and recall information.

Since this is not a memory book, per se, we won't dive deeper into every memory technique. I do want to share with you a memory technique using the Loci Method, which is on the list above.

The Loci method involves pairing what you have to remember with a familiar location. Think of a place you know like the back of your hand—a place you wouldn't even have to think about. This could be your house, your walk to work or school, or it could even be bigger, like a city.

Let's say you had seven grocery items to remember. With this method, you can remember a lot more than seven things, but we'll just keep it at seven to keep it simple.

Let's say the seven items are:

1) Milk 2) Eggs 3) Avocados 4) Beans 5) Syrup
6) Coffee 7) Broccoli

Now, the idea is to pick your familiar place and match the first 7 locations with your grocery list.

I'll use my home. I'll start in the living room / kitchen area.

1) fireplace 2) TV 3) sofa 4) pool table 5) sliding doors
6) counter 7) refrigerator

Take note that your location should always be the same order all the time, so the order is something you have memorized and not something you have to think hard to remember.

We are not done yet. We now have to associate and create a mental picture with our grocery list.

Here's how that works:

1. Milk & Fireplace—so what I would do here is picture milk instead of flames for the fire inside the fireplace. I would watch the white milk spark and crackle just like a fire.
2. Eggs & TV—Maybe I would picture a carton of eggs being thrown at the TV and yolk dripping off the TV and the TV just being a slimy mess.
3. Avocados & Sofa—I could think of smearing avocado all over the sofa, as if it were a taco instead of a sofa.
4. Beans & Pool Table—That's easy. I could pretend the balls on the pool table are beans instead of the actual pool table balls. The balls on the table would all be black (or pinto colored) and they would have numbers on them like pool table balls do.
5. Syrup & Sliding Doors—Syrup is slippery. I could be oiling the doors with syrup. Or I can use letter association. Syrup and Sliding Doors—both begin with the letter *S*.
6. Coffee & Counter—There's another alliteration with the Cs, or if I wanted to visualize something, I could envision 100 coffee cups on the counter, filled to the brim with coffee.
7. Broccoli & Refrigerator—Picture a huge broccoli growing from the base of the fridge and towering over it.

You want to not only create a mental picture, but you want to think of the picture as very specific, and you want to turn the ordinary into something extraordinary. For my example for number six, the coffee, I didn't just think of one coffee cup; I pictured hundreds of cups on the counter with coffee in them. You want to exaggerate the picture in your mind because this is going to help with the recollection process.

So why are we talking about memory in a book about reading faster? Well, because as I said earlier, it's not about the words just flying into your ears. You want to have a way to ingest the information, store it in your brain, and talk about it at a later time—otherwise, what's the purpose?

If you are using The BuzzRead Method with a fiction book, it's a lot easier to envision what's going on in the story. You can place the characters, the location, what the characters look like, and their surroundings. It is important to note that you do need to be actively engaged, listening, and following along, even if you are reading fiction.

When it comes to non-fiction, things can get a little more complicated. You might have to remember terms, rules, orders, lists, methods, systems, and acronyms. Just because you are getting through the material—and getting through it fast—that doesn't guarantee you are going to retain one hundred percent of the information.

After we set up the device for The BuzzRead Method, we are going to talk more about how to retain the information you read, and I am going to give you some tips that work to do this.

First, let's go ahead and set up our device.

# CHAPTER 9

# SETTING UP YOUR DEVICE FOR THE BUZZREAD METHOD

NOW THAT WE KNOW:

- What The BuzzRead Method is
- The important components of this method and why it's different from audiobooks
- How our brain works to recall and remember information...

We are ready to set it up on our electronic devices.

You can use The BuzzRead Method on any device you choose. I prefer to do mine right on my iPhone 6 Plus. You can do this on an iPad, tablets with the accessibility function present, specific Kindle devices, and on any kind of smartphone that also has an accessibility function. You can also use it on a laptop or desktop computer, which we will talk about later.

## APPLE DEVICE SET UP

**Here is how you can get Text To Speech to work from your iPhone or iPad, using this new feature.**

1. Go into Settings.

## 2. Choose General.

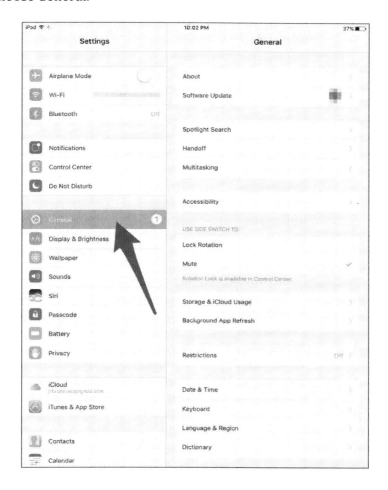

## 3. Under General, choose Accessibility

## 4. Choose Speech

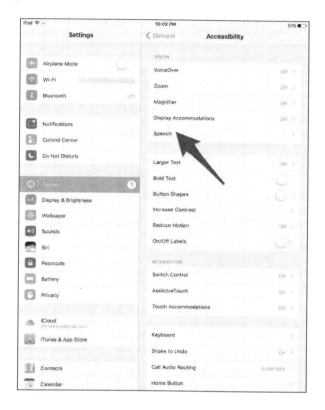

## 5. Under Speech, choose Speak Screen

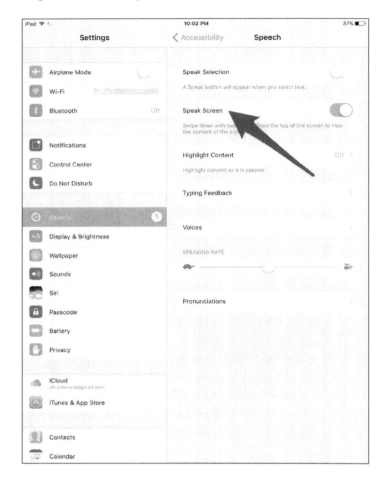

6. Exit Settings and open your Kindle app on your device

1.  While on a page, swipe down with two fingers from the top of
    the screen to hear the content of the screen

## ANDROID DEVICE SET UP

### How to get TTS on Android devices to read out loud to you

If you have a lot of readings to do but don't have a lot of time to sit and read, Text Speech is an excellent option.

1. Go into Settings

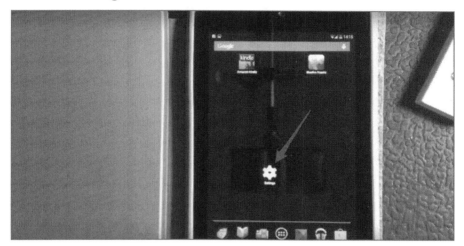

## 2. Scroll down to the bottom and select Accessibility

## 3. Select Talkback

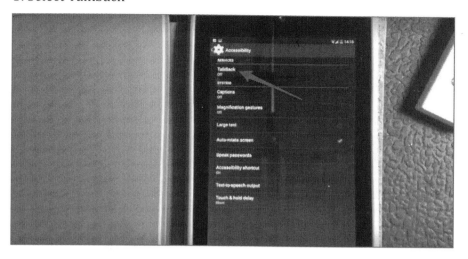

## 4. Press on the Off button above

### 5. Press on OK and Talkback will switch on

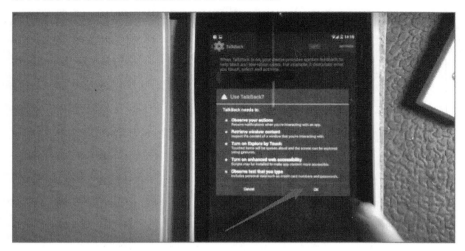

### 6. Exit the Settings and open your Kindle app on your device

7. While on a page, swipe down with two fingers from the top of the screen to hear the content of the screen

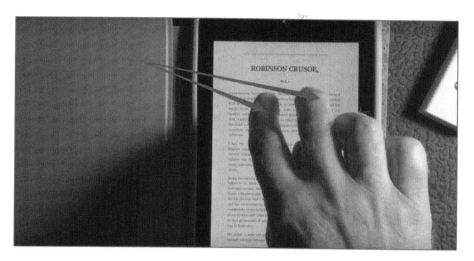

8. Once you get your tap speed and control speed, you are ready. Always remember to turn off TalkBack before you close down the device; otherwise, you have to start double-clicking when you want to use it again.

## KINDLE DEVICE SET UP

I don't use a Kindle device to read books. I mostly use my phone or my iPad. I am actually in the minority because statistics from the Book Expo Event in Chicago in 2016 stated that the majority of people use e-readers like the Kindle to read, and actually, many people are beginning to express a preference for physical books again. Go Figure!

In doing my research to help as many people with different devices, I found that Kindle devices, including the paperwhite, which I recently purchased, does not have the ability to do text to speech (TTS). TTS does not work with any of Amazon's Kindle e-readers.

The only way to use text-to-speech on Kindle books is to use a Fire tablet, Fire Phone, or one of the older model E-Ink Kindles that Amazon doesn't make anymore, such as the Kindle Touch, Kindle

Keyboard, Kindle 2, and Kindle DX. Those devices are only available secondhand these days.

The only way to make use of TTS when using a Kindle e-reader is to use a Fire tablet or a Fire Phone. This TTS function will be in your settings. This is difficult to demonstrate because the process will vary with different generations of devices. The function is called Read Aloud on some and Read Text on others. It's in there, and it all means the same thing. As I'll also explain a bit later, if you are having trouble, you can always visit **http://youtube.com** and do a search, and you'll find many videos to help you get started.

I have been doing some online research and have read that Fire tablets use IVONA's text-to-speech voices, and they sound surprisingly pleasant. There are a bunch of additional voices that can be installed, as well, including a number of foreign-language voices. These are accessible from the settings menu under language.

So, it's kind of a bummer that it doesn't work on the traditional—and newer—Kindle e-readers, but if you really want to use the method, you will need to use any Apple device or Samsung smartphone or one of the specific Kindle devices listed above.

You are all set to use The BuzzRead Method! How exciting! Let's get into the details of the functions to pace your reading.

| Action Step |
| --- |
| Go ahead and fire up your text to speech (TTS) feature on your reading device. You can practice by reading the rest of this book using The BuzzRead Method. |
| Don't stop reading this book yet even though you know the method! There are still important details to learn about this method in order to make it work great for you, so read on. |

# CHAPTER 10

# ACTIVATING, CHANGING YOUR SPEED, AND PAUSING

AS STATED IN THE previous instructions above, to activate the text to speech, you need to place two fingers at the top of the screen and swipe down. It doesn't always work at first because you need just the right finesse when swiping, but you will get the hang of it. When the voice starts to read, you might find you want to make some adjustments to the speed.

I created some videos to walk you through the process of setting up your device for The BuzzRead Method. It's all free and available right here: **http://debbiedrum.com/buzzreadvids**.

The best part about The BuzzRead Method is how quickly you will see an improvement in your ability to follow along and listen faster, which will get you through the material faster.

With text to speech, you can adjust the speed to go very slowly or extremely fast. You will find there is a speed where the words become incomprehensible. You need to find a speed you're comfortable with, which will be different for everyone.

I can normally keep up with a speed that's faster than double-time, but for certain business books that have key concepts to understand, I like to listen a bit slower. I tend to visualize what's going on in fiction books at a much faster speed. I can also listen to non-fiction material that I'm already familiar with where I'm not learning it for the first time at a setting that's a little faster than double speed. The voice goes very fast, but as long as you keep following along and keep listening, comprehension is not a problem.

On the Apple devices, the speed is represented as a turtle and a bunny. You press the bunny if you want to speed up, and you press the turtle if you want to slow down (see picture below). Makes sense, right? Unfortunately, there is no percentage meter or slider that allows you to track how fast you are going, so you'll just have to guestimate, and keep changing the setting until you find a speed you're comfortable

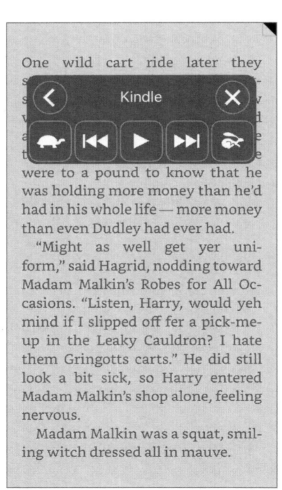

with.

Finally, the play button becomes the pause button when it's activated. I would recommend pausing when you need to—whether to define a word or re-listen to key points. Anytime you want to go back to a certain point in the book, you must close the TTS by clicking the *X* button, and then turn it back on by swiping two fingers downward from the top of the screen.

| Action Step |
| --- |
| Practice activating the text to speech function by placing two fingers at the top of the screen and swiping downward. If you are having trouble, go to http://debbiedrum.com/buzzreadvids, and you can watch my demonstration. |
| Test out different speeds with text to speech on your device. |
| Find your comfort level. This most likely will vary, depending on the type of book you're reading. For example, you might be able to go much faster with a fiction book than you can with a business, non-fiction book. |

# CHAPTER 11

# WORKING WITH PDFS

YOU MIGHT FIND YOU have a PDF you want to read, and you want to use The BuzzRead Method. Well, you're in luck because you can! In case you are not aware, PDF stands for Portable Document Format, and you can tell a file is a PDF file when it ends in .pdf.

Working The BuzzRead Method is simple with a PDF file.

There are two ways you can do this.

## SIMPLY CLICK AND OPEN THE PDF

If you click on a PDF document, you can open it up just by clicking on it, and it should open in a PDF format. Most smartphones and devices will open PDF documents in a web browser. After you've opened the file, you can just swipe your device from the top to activate the text to speech and the device will start reading your content.

Personally, I don't like reading PDFs from my phone because you can't adjust the size to make it properly fit on the screen, and sometimes, you have to zoom in and out quite a bit to read, which can become annoying. It also doesn't look like a nicely formatted book when you open it as a PDF directly.

When reading a PDF in a web browser, you can't bookmark or highlight, either. More on bookmarking and highlighting later on.

That's why I prefer the second option, which is...

## OPEN THE PDF IN YOUR READING APP

This next option to read a PDF is a multi-step process, but it works great.

First, I have some bad news. You can choose to open a PDF in your Kindle app; however, I tested the TTS option on my iPhone to use The BuzzRead Method, and, unfortunately, it says "no speak-able content can be found on the screen" when you activate the TTS. However, the good news is, if you choose the option to open the PDF in the iBook app, it *does* work! Simply open the PDF in your iBook app, and you're good to go.

That's great if you have an Apple device, but what do you do if you use some other brand of device?

In order to work The BuzzRead Method using the Kindle app, there are 3 options we can take.

### Option 1: Send Your PDF File To Your Kindle App

This method works like a charm to read PDFs on your Kindle app and use The BuzzRead Method. You want to get the PDF into your Kindle App (as opposed to just opening the PDF with your Kindle app).

There's a couple of ways to get files on your Kindle App. The first is simply email the PDF to your Kindle email.

A Kindle email address is attached to each Kindle device or app. You can find your Kindle email address by visiting the "Manage your Devices" page from your Amazon account.

- Login to your Amazon.com account. From there, click on the "Your Account" button in the toolbar toward the top of the page.

- Click "Manage Your Content and Devices" link.

- Now, you'll see three tabs toward the top of the page. "Your Content," "Your Devices," and "Settings." Click on the Settings Tab.

- *Scroll down, and you will see an email address associated with each Kindle device you have.

- Open an email and attach the PDF and hit send.

- When you are on your Kindle app on your device, you might have to hit the sync button, and you will see the PDF on your device. You will be good to go at this point.

*Note:* You need to send the email to the correct device in order to get it on your account. If you are confused about which device is which, simply go to your account on the actual Kindle app, go to "Settings" and in the settings, you will see: Send To Kindle Email Address, and you will get the correct email address for your specific device.

## Option 2: Connect Your Kindle Device to Your Computer

Another way to get a PDF into your Kindle app is to connect your Kindle device to your computer, and transfer the file.

Instructions for Option 1 and Option 2 can be found at: http://debbiedrum.com/wikipdfinstructions

## Option 3: Download an app called: The E-book Converter

Here's the final option to use The BuzzRead Method with a PDF on your Kindle App.

The E-book Converter is an app that costs $2.99 (USD) but the price is well worth it because it works great.

The app will convert your PDF files to a .mobi file—the file type you need to read your book on the Kindle app.

The app icon looks like this:

Here are the steps to convert your PDF, and read it inside of the Kindle app to activate TTS.

## Step 1: Access The PDF

When you have the PDF open, there should be some kind of Export option. On the iPhone and other Apple devices, it's called Export, and the symbol has a box with an arrow. I usually save my files to my phone using the Dropbox app, which is just a file storage system. There are a bunch of ways to store files, such as the Apple Cloud and Google storage. I prefer Dropbox.

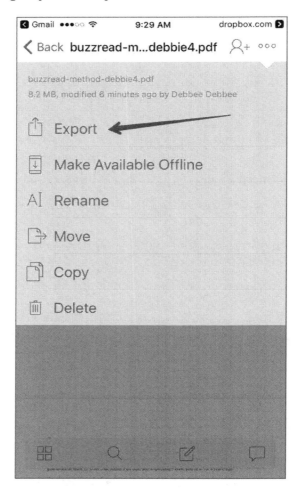

## Step 2: Click Export and then select Open In

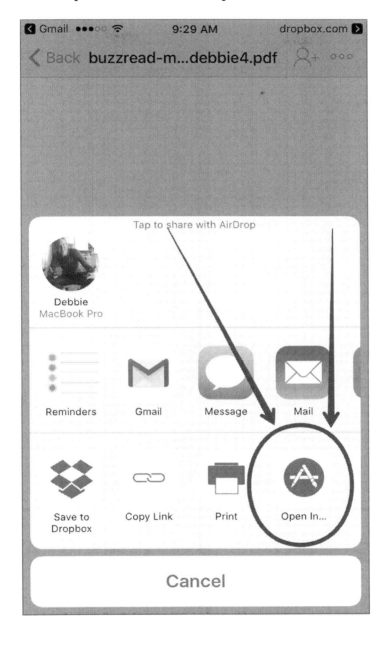

**Step 3: Select Import with Ebook Converter**

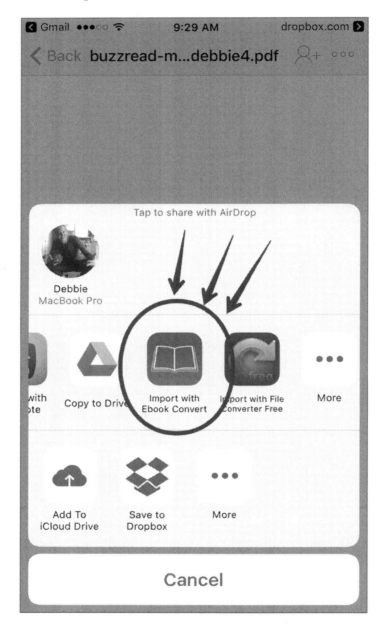

**Step 4: Convert the file to MOBI (Kindle Format)**

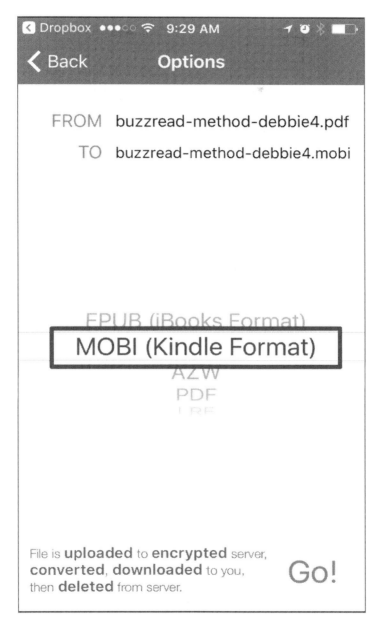

**Step 5: Once the file is finished converting, select Open With:**

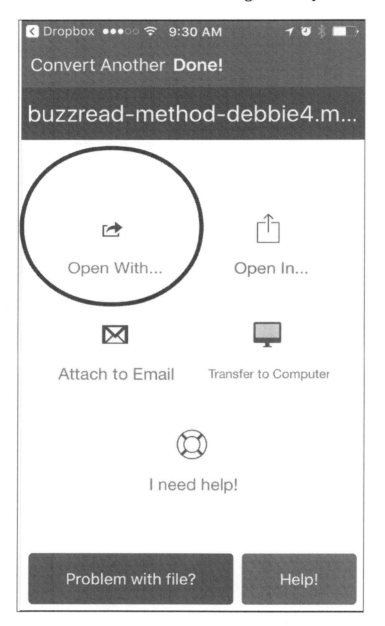

**Step 6: Open with the Kindle app and enjoy reading!**

As you can see, there are a few steps involved, but once you get the hang of it, it's easy. The whole process takes less than five minutes, and afterward, you have a great working solution.

Again, you need to choose one option from above because PDFs are unreadable on the Kindle app, and you won't be able to use the TTS or The BuzzRead Method if you don't convert the file first.

Warning: One annoying part of the process that sometimes happens with PDFs is the device will read footers and page numbers. This might be part of the conversion process and why this happens, but it definitely interrupts the flow of the read, as you can imagine. This is something you have to just get used to or somehow fix in the original file. The only way to fix it is if you have a .doc version of the file and remove all the headers and footers and then convert it back to a PDF without that info. I tend to just leave it and live with it, but you can decide what to do for your own comfort and reading enjoyment.

By now, you should be well-equipped to set up The BuzzRead Method using PDFs on your electronic device.

| Action Step |
|---|
| Pick one way to get comfortable getting your PDFs onto your Kindle App. They are all pretty simple, but it's good to get used to one way, so it doesn't take you too long. |
| Test it out to make sure it works before you go mobile. |

# CHAPTER 12

# THE BUZZREAD METHOD ON YOUR DESKTOP

UP UNTIL NOW, WE'VE been talking about mobile devices, such as smartphones, tablets, and Kindle readers. Now, let's go over how you can use TTS on your desktop or laptop.

There may come a time when you want to read on your computer, and you'll want to get through the material quicker than you can read on your own. Sure, it's good to have your content on the go, but you might not need to do that all the time. So let's talk about some ways you can use The BuzzRead Method right from your computer.

Did you know you can read Kindle books on your computer? There are a couple ways to do it. You can download the Kindle app, or you can use the Kindle Cloud Reader. Simply Google "Kindle Cloud Reader," and you will be taken to a sign-in page, and all your books will appear on your computer.

With the Kindle Cloud Reader, you will notice you can't select any text to copy information. You can only select text to highlight or make notes. That's it. Most TTS software on a desktop or laptop requires you to select the text, and that's what prompts the TTS to know what to read back to you. Since you can only select text for highlighting purposes on the Kindle Cloud Reader, the computer won't realize the text is selected, and therefore, it won't read the text aloud, and The BuzzRead Method won't work.

Your other option is to download the actual Kindle app on your computer from your app store, and that is where the magic happens. When you open the Kindle app on your computer, you will be able to select text, and then use your computer's TTS to read the text back to you.

## BUILT-IN TEXT TO SPEECH

Most desktops and laptops these days have built-in TTS. This feature comes standard on every Apple and Chromebook Device.

I won't be able to demonstrate every single device here, but again, simply head over to **http://youtube.com,** and type in your device name and TTS, and you will find a slew of videos demonstrating how to enable this function.

Turning on TTS is usually a very simple process. On a Mac, you just head over to System Preferences => Accessibility => Speech => and then select "speak selected text when the key is pressed."

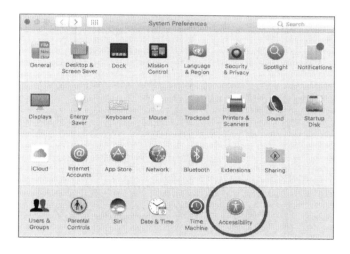

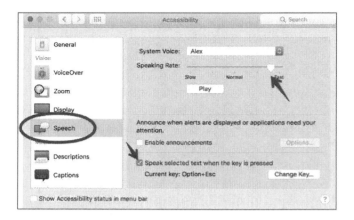

You can control the read speed with the slider.

As you can see, you need to select the text on your computer, and then press the keystroke to activate the TTS—in my example, on my computer, the keystroke is Option + Esc. The keystroke to activate is the same keystroke to terminate the TTS.

## TOOLS

If, for some reason, you don't want to use your computer's TTS option, there are many tools that do TTS, and I will reference two.

1. **Natural Reader: https://www.naturalreaders.com/ download.html**. This tool was recommended to me by one of my subscribers. I tested it out, and it works great. It's a free tool, and it's available for both Macs and PCs. There is a paid option for syncing content, among other features, but the free version works just fine.
2. **Chrome Apps:** There are many Google Chrome apps you can install—for free or paid—that will read content back to you.

I use an app called Select and Speak—Text To Speech (SpeakIt). This app sits in your Chrome toolbar, and you can activate it when you want. It looks like this:

You do not need this tool if you have built-in text to speech on your device already.

If you don't use Chrome or you use another browser, such as Internet Explorer, Safari, or Firefox, simply go to **http://google.com**, and Google the term "text to speech [Your browser]."

There are so many options. I can't review them all; otherwise, I would never finish this book. I highly recommend the built-in TTS on your device because with the improved technology it works really well. In fact, I used my computer's TTS to proofread this entire book. One strategy to proofread a book before you send it to an editor is to read the book out loud. Reading a book out loud is exhausting and tiring. I simply let the computer read the book out loud to me, and it worked great!

You can't beat the time we live in now. It's pretty extraordinary.

## USING THE BUZZREAD METHOD WITH PHYSICAL BOOKS AND PRINT OUTS

Obviously, The BuzzRead Method is a new-age method to read faster. It doesn't apply to physical books the way other speed-reading methods do. However, if you have a physical copy of your book or a printout copy, you can always implement The BuzzRead Method, and set up your mobile device or desktop computer and follow along with your physical copy. For this you will need a digital copy as well as the physical copy of the book.

I understand some folks love physical books for various reasons. One of my subscribers said she sees the text better on a printed copy. So, you can have the best of both worlds as long as you have the digital copy of the book, so you can utilize the technology even with a physical book.

Now you have a way to use The BuzzRead Method, whether you are mobile or at your computer. Wherever you are, the method doesn't change. Please follow the exact method I teach throughout this book. Next, we are going to take a look at some of the traps and pitfalls you could encounter with this method. Don't worry; I am going to help you avoid those to guarantee your success.

| Review |
| --- |
| You can read your Kindle books on a desktop or laptop computer using Kindle Cloud Reader or the Kindle app, but you can only use The BuzzRead Method with the Kindle app, as you cannot select text with the Kindle Cloud Reader. |
| Most modern desktops and laptops have Text To Speech; you simply have to activate it, and you're all set. |
| Other applications, such as Natural Reader and certain Chrome apps allow you to enable Text To Speech for webpages, PDFs, and documents. |
| You can technically use The BuzzRead Method with a physical book, but you also need a copy of the digital book. Simply turn on your TTS, and then use the physical book to follow along. |

# CHAPTER 13

# ABOUT...THE VOICE

WHEN YOUR DEVICE READS back to you, it's not going to sound like a human. This is another reason The BuzzRead Method is different from audiobooks. With audiobooks, you have a human narrator reading to you. This could be a good thing or a bad thing, depending on your perspective. Narrators can make or break book sales and book enjoyment for listeners. If you don't like the narrator, you might not enjoy the overall experience. On the other hand, if you love the narrator, you will buy every book that narrator reads! Narrators help sell books.

With The BuzzRead Method, on an Apple device, you will get one voice, which kind of sounds like Siri. Let's call her voice Siri for simplicity's sake. Siri's voice and narration style is a lot more consistent than a human narrator, making it easier for your brain to focus on the content and ideas instead of the voice.

In my opinion, I prefer having one voice read all my reading material to me—and not a lot of different voices like you'll find in audiobooks. I think this is a plus because then you can grow numb to the way it sounds, and focus on the content of what you are reading. It's a component that should not affect your process at all. If you don't like a robot reading to you, you may not enjoy The BuzzRead Method, but if you learn to love it—or just get used to it—then the method will work very well for you.

You can install other voices on your devices, but some of the additional voices do tend to take up room on your device, so you might not want to do that, or proceed with caution. Personally, I went with the default Siri-like voice, and as I said, I enjoy it and prefer using one voice for everything.

As I said above, Siri does take some getting used to, especially for Kindle books, where there might be many words that have a dash in them. These words end with a dash on one line and then the rest of the word continues on the next line. Oftentimes, that's the case for many words in a Kindle book. The voice reads those words in an awkward way, and it sounds off sometimes—the word doesn't sound like the actual word because it's divided. If you are following along, as you should be with The BuzzRead Method, then you shouldn't have too much of a problem understanding the word in context, and eventually, you will get used to this.

One other minor thing is that the TTS doesn't always pause long enough after periods, so it may rush into the next sentence quicker than you might expect.

The odd pronunciation of separated words and the lack of proper pausing after a period are the only issues I've found with the process. Again, I grew accustomed to these little glitches, and it shouldn't be hard for you to do the same.

One more funny note and a strange observation…

The default Siri has an American accent, with no strong hint to where in America she is from, except when she says the word "talk." She says the word *talk* in a very strong, New York accent—so it sounds more like "tawk." This is very funny to me. Many other words with an "a" she also says in a New York accent…like "tawll" (tall). Listen for these words, and you'll have a good laugh from time to time.

Next, the strange observation I made that is evident more on my iMac TTS is Alex's voice (which is the default American accent reader) breathes when he reads. I am not quite sure why a computer reading to you needs to take breaths because it's not a living thing. I don't know…you can ponder that along with me. ☺

# CHAPTER 14

# How To Skim
# For Optimal Results

WE TALKED ABOUT SKIMMING or following along with the content while Siri reads the text to you and about how this is important for retention, comprehension, and improved overall reading (the traditional way of reading). The process works like magic when practiced correctly.

The skimming process is very easy, but I want to tell you how to practice it for optimal results.

While Siri reads the text to you, your eyes should be following along. Simply go back and forth, and follow along each line. You *do not* want to read each word in your head or sub-vocalize because if you have this habit, we want to do our best to reduce and even eliminate sub-vocalization.

The BuzzRead Method will help you to recognize words as you see them without having to say them in your head. This is what develops for fast readers over time, and it will develop for you. When you follow along and avoid sub-vocalizing, you will be practicing a form of skimming but actually fully comprehending the text.

When you are speed-reading, skimming is a learned skill. The intention is to grasp the overall feeling of the content without reading every single word or every single line of the content. While skimming is beneficial to get through the content faster, you will miss some details. It's impossible to catch everything and skim at the same time. However, with The BuzzRead Method, because Siri is reading *all* of the text to you, it's hard to miss detail. You can always stop the reading, repeat it, or have Siri read slower, so you can grasp the content better. That's why I prefer The BuzzRead Method over skimming or speed-reading.

Even though we are not fully skimming when we use The BuzzRead Method because the full text is read to us, it is still important to know how to skim. This will come in handy when you are reading the traditional way.

Eventually, you will want to use a combination of The BuzzRead Method plus skimming to get through books and content even faster and smarter. This is where knowing how to skim read will come in handy.

## How To Skim Read

Skimming is a reading strategy that helps us find the main idea of a text fast.

Skimming helps us:

1. Know what kind of text we are reading, whether it's fiction, non-fiction, news, an article, etc.
2. Get the main idea fast, especially if the text is long
3. Recap something we have already read, instead of having to re-read the entire book, article, etc.
4. Determine if we want to read the text at all—perhaps the text might not be useful for us to read
5. Get through material faster if we don't have a lot of time.

The idea of skimming is to read only the most important parts.

Here is what we read when the goal is to skim through content:

- Title
- Pictures
- Subheadings
- First Paragraph
- First sentence of other paragraphs
- Last Paragraph
- Bold, italics, and underlines
- Bulleted Lists

By reading the above parts of the content, you will get a good idea of what's important enough for you to get more detail about and what you might want to pass over.

So, how does skim reading fit in with The BuzzRead Method?

## WHAT TO EXPECT AFTER 30 DAYS USING THE BUZZREAD METHOD

If you follow The BuzzRead Method, you will read and get through more books faster and easier. That's a given. You will also start to see improvement in your everyday reading, and you will begin to see you can read faster in general. You will start to notice the benefits after practicing the method with about ten books.

Next, you will want to incorporate skim reading with The BuzzRead Method. In other words, you will still want to follow along with the text, but you might not want to or have to read every single part of every book. So you will use your skimming skills to scan the text to see if you have to read certain sections or chapters.

Here's an example:

Let's say you are researching different types of techniques and strategies to grow an organic garden. Now, because you can read books fast with The BuzzRead Method, you have three books you'd like to read for guidance on this topic. The books might have some overlapping content that you don't need to read three times. Perhaps they each have similar suggestions on where to get soil and how to lay the soil. You don't have to read the same information over and over.

Therefore, you can skip certain parts of the content to save time. When you come across new information, you can then fire up The BuzzRead Method, and get going with reading the content.

I was recently reading a book about developing good habits to improve your life and career. There were sections I bypassed completely because I was familiar with the information. The book was fairly long, and in an effort to finish it quickly, I skipped the sections that contained content I already knew. To do this, I looked at the subheadings, lists, bold text, and bulleted sections of the book. This allowed me to avoid wasting time reading parts that were defining terms I already knew.

This is how you combine the strategies for optimal results. When you get to the stage where you are able to skip through content you already know, it's a great feeling!

# CHAPTER 15

# AVOIDING TRAPS
# AND PITFALLS

AS WITH ANY METHOD, there are benefits and pitfalls to The BuzzRead Method. I hope you clearly see all of the benefits because it will help you concentrate and get through books and reading material faster. However, getting through the material doesn't mean you will be grasping all of the information you are consuming. There is a tendency to feel a sense of achievement when you accomplish a task of, let's say, reading one hundred pages in one sitting, but how much of that hundred pages did you actually understand and remember? If I asked you questions about what you read, would you score one hundred percent? Eighty? If you went through the content without retaining the information, then the method has failed you.

So essentially, the trap is feeling you are successful because you went through the material, yet you didn't really accomplish much because you didn't absorb the material.

Retention is important. Remembering what you read and making it stick is crucial. Obviously, it might be hard to remember every little fact, but you do want to remember main points, so you can speak about them later on without having to reference back to the book all the time.

One of the reasons people still love physical books is because they can easily refer back to previously marked pages—the "dog ears" some book readers despise—as well as any notes and underlining you might have made in the book. Basically, you can easily return to important sections you wanted to reference later because the book is easily accessible.

You might be surprised to realize you can do this with electronic books, too. Reading with the Kindle app allows you to do this very easily.

Here's the first retention trick.

## THE BOOKMARK AND HIGHLIGHT RETENTION TECHNIQUE

You have the ability to bookmark any page on the Kindle app. I use the bookmark function to remember where I left off, but I also use it for pages I want to be able to reference easily later on.

Bookmarking is easy—it's on the top right when you tap on the page—and it looks like a bookmark. See the image below.

I also use the highlight feature. You can highlight passages in four different colors.

To get to the highlight section, tap the screen.

To highlight, simply hold down your finger on the section you want to highlight, and then you will see this menu come up. Select the text to highlight.

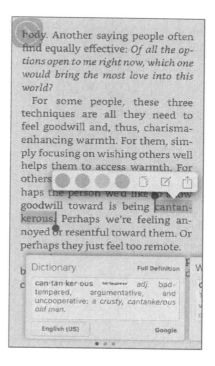

As a side note, when you select text, the dictionary tool will also come up. That's another reason I *love* reading electronically. I wish the ability to simply highlight text had been available to me when I was younger. I am sure my vocabulary would be more extensive because I would have taken advantage of the simplicity of looking up words I didn't know. Okay, opening up a dictionary isn't too hard a task, but dictionaries aren't always accessible. I don't know about you, but when I was traveling on the subway in NYC as a teenager, and I was reading a book on the train, chances were very slim that I was carrying a dictionary around with me.

So, I digress...getting back to highlighting.

You can color-coordinate your highlights if you choose. It's a neat feature.

Now, here's the main benefit of highlighting.

When you press this button on the bottom left (the one that looks like a bunch of boxes):

The view like this should come up:

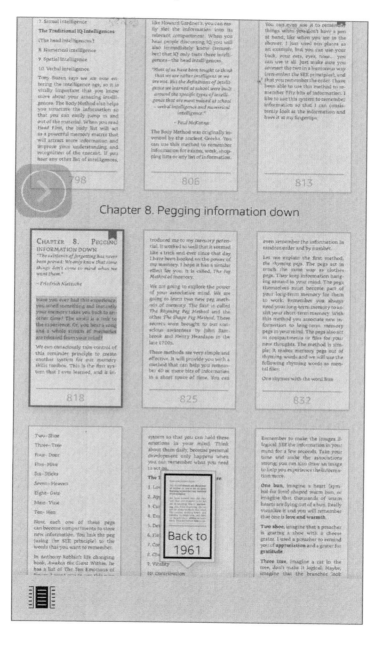

Do you see how you can easily pinpoint highlighted areas? You can highlight in different colors and have your own color system. I highly recommend implementing this practice because you'll be going through the material fast, and you want to be able to get back to important parts quickly. You can also make notes, but I haven't found the note feature very useful because highlighting the material seems to work just as well and serves the same purpose.

Here's a better note-taking tactic...

## RETENTION OVERBOARD TECHNIQUE

I call this the *Retention Overboard Technique* because you will be going the extra mile to retain information if you do this.

After you read for your allotted amount of time, open a document, and take notes on what you've just read. You can write freely from memory, and you can always go back and re-listen to something you want to get more details about. Writing strengthens the connection with the new material you've just learned.

You don't want to write down everything you read—only the material that's important to you and that you believe is imperative you don't forget. If you are reading a fiction book for fun, chances are you will not have to refer to specific details later. But if you are studying for something or if it's a business book with key takeaway points you want to put into practice later, you might want to take notes and have a more concrete place—physically and mentally—to keep the information.

I normally open a Google Doc and write my notes there. I usually write key points with bullets, and oftentimes, information isn't in order, and I'll even leave misspellings. This is for my reference, only, and no one else will see it unless I decide to share my notes for some reason.

I like Google Docs because I can access the notes from everywhere, even my smartphone. If you are mobile and still want to take notes, you will be able to do that.

Evernote is another great program for notetaking. You can have different notebooks for different topics, and you are easily able to find files with tags you assign to them. It makes staying organized super easy—which is the entire purpose of Evernote.

The basic version of Evernote is free, but there is a paid version as well if you want more features. Evernote is also a tool you can use on the go with the mobile app. If you write a note on your desktop or your mobile, the note will sync to your account, so everything is current no matter where you use it.

Here's a sample of the notes I take.

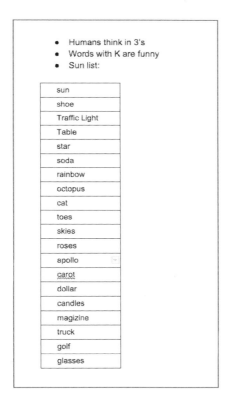

I usually like to take my notes when I am at a desktop or laptop. That's just my personal preference because I can type a whole lot faster on a regular keyboard.

Remember, these notes are for you, and they should be easily accessible, so you can write notes anytime, anywhere.

When reviewing your notes, you can use functions like bold, italics, headings, and different colors of highlights. You will eventually develop your own system for structuring your documents, so they're easy for you to understand when you need to read them at a later date.

Here's one final retention trick I'll share with you:

## THE TEACH-BACK TECHNIQUE

When I was in college, I was always in a study group. Not because I was unable to study alone—I could do that just fine. I joined study groups for a few reasons.

1. **To turn something boring into a little bit of fun.** I remember my study groups were a lot of work, but we had some good times, too.

2. **To kick myself into doing the work.** I am and always was self-motivated, but making appointments to meet people at a certain time definitely forces you to go and to do the work that needed to be done.

3. **To study by teaching.** Now, this was the main reason I loved study groups. One of the best ways to learn something is to teach what you have learned to someone else. When you speak the material out loud, it builds a stronger association with the content you need to remember. Not only does it remain in your brain, but you also develop certain memories about the content after you teach it, because it's very similar to recalling a story with pictures, which is the best way to remember something.

For example, I'll never forget when I was studying economics in college with my friend, and we were learning about the federal reserve and how that works. I can't tell you much about that topic now, but I'll never forget the crazy lady stick figure with the messy hair and triangle dress we drew on the chalkboard to depict "the fed" and how they governed and made the rules. It was not only helpful to envision that stick figure, but it was also hysterical at the same time.

| Review |
|---|
| You will be going through a lot of material very fast. The last thing you want to do is feel a sense of accomplishment without actually retaining the information you have consumed. |
| The first retention trick involves bookmarking, so you can quickly reference important material on your device. Tapping on the box in the lower left-hand corner in the Kindle app will allow you to see all your bookmarks at a glance. |
| The second retention trick is the highlighting tool. You highlight text by selecting the text you want to highlight with your finger. Again, selecting the box on the bottom left will also allow you to see your highlighted content easily and refer back to things very quickly. |
| For ultimate retention, you can use the Retention Overboard Technique, where you have a separate place you take notes immediately after you read. Writing things down will help you remember the content. |
| Make it easy to reference your notes at all times—including when you are mobile. I recommend Google Docs or Evernote. Both programs are in the Cloud, so you can access the latest information on your document at all times and across various devices. |
| Whenever you can, however, you should try to teach what you are learning to someone else. This will help you voice what you have learned and will also create something memorable when you are attempting to retrieve the content at a later time. |

# CHAPTER 16

# MEASURING AND TRACKING YOUR PROGRESS AND SUCCESS

ONE OF THE GREATEST aspects of The BuzzRead Method is that you can easily manage and track your success and progress. Take note of the image below:

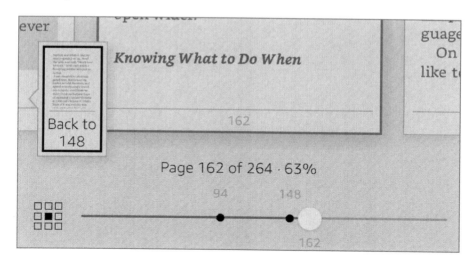

See the bottom where it says Page 162 of 264 and 63%?

This is how you can easily time manage how fast you are getting through a book. So if you wanted to give yourself a deadline of four days, you would make sure you read at least twenty-five percent of the book each day. If there was a three hundred-page book you wanted to get through in three days, then you'd just have to go through one hundred pages per day. How awesome is that? I love this aspect because nothing is left to the unknown, and you can structure your reading, so it fits into your day.

The time it takes you to get through the material will also vary. As I said earlier, when you first start The BuzzRead Method, you will want to have Siri read to you at a normal pace. As you get better and better at this, you will want to pick up the pace and go faster. When you go faster, you will finish in less time. You will start to learn how much time it takes you to get through an allotted amount of reading material in a specified time.

# CHAPTER 17

# DEDICATION AND PRACTICING THE SYSTEM

AS WITH ANYTHING WORTH accomplishing, you need to practice this method. As you practice The BuzzRead Method. you are going to be reading books fast and actually finishing books you wanted to read.

The *real* practice comes into play when you skim along while Siri reads to you. You *have* to do this, and it is essential to the practice. There should be no ifs, ands, or buts about it. This is the secret sauce to what is going to make you a better and faster reader, even when you read the traditional way. It all works together.

You should practice no less than thirty minutes a day. Dedicating thirty minutes a day to reading is a very realistic goal and a modest effort.

Here are four things to think about.

**1, Mix It Up with Non-fiction and Fiction:** If you want to read non-fiction and business books, that's great! However, mixing in a bit of fiction will add some levity and relaxation to your reading. This will also give you practice reading all different types of books.

**2. Read More Than One Book at Once:** The beautiful thing about The BuzzRead Method is you will read more in less time, so you will have more time to read if you want to do so! While you can switch it up between non-fiction and fiction, you can also read a couple books at once. You can be the one to decide how many books you can handle at one time. I won't give you any suggestions here because everyone is different, and it's a matter of personal preference and, ultimately, how much time you have.

Currently, I am reading two books—one business/self-help book and one fiction book. That's comfortable for me and my time constraints, but you might have different needs and schedule issues. Reading one book at a time is just fine, too.

**3. Read More Than Once a Day:** In the beginning, I would aim to read for thirty minutes a day. You may have a tougher time working through some non-fiction books, while some fiction books might be more of a breeze.

Depending on how much time you have to dedicate to reading, you can read multiple times a day—perhaps in the morning and again in the afternoon or evening.

You will find reading much more enjoyable, and you will want to read more than once a day. Sometimes, it will be necessary to take breaks. If you are reading a book that requires a lot of brain power, it might take you slightly longer to get through. You may also find if you stretched your limit, you will want to take a nap, which, if you have the time, is perfectly fine. In the beginning, even after the first thirty days of doing this method, you will get tired, and you'll have to work to increase your stamina in order to read longer.

I like to make mini goals for how much I want to read every day. I do this by looking at the percentage of the book on the meter the Kindle app provides (discussed in the previous chapter). I don't stop until I hit my goal. If I don't hit my goal in one sitting, I make certain I schedule more time for later in the day. Admittedly, sometimes I miss my goal entirely on a certain day, but that's okay because I just pick up the next day and restart. It's so important to have measurable goals, and I would also suggest tracking your progress.

**4. Learn Something New or Hone a New Skill:** When you are learning or studying something new, this type of reading will typically take you longer to get through.

Trust me, you are going to want to read a lot of books at once, and it might be hard to juggle them all, especially if you have limited time. If you want to learn something new, I would advise you to dedicate a small amount of time per day for this.

For example, I am currently reading two books at once, but I've incorporated a third piece of reading material about copywriting—a skill I want to get better at. Copywriting isn't something you can learn everything about overnight. It is more of a lifelong process and study.

If I make it a habit to study an aspect of copywriting every day for at least fifteen minutes per day, I know that over time—even within a month—I will be tremendously better at copywriting. Isn't that pretty amazing? Only fifteen minutes per day adds up to a little over seven and a half hours per month. Times that by twelve, and that's ninety hours I'll have devoted to studying this new skill over the course of a year.

*Wow*! That totals up to a pretty impressive amount of time in the grand scheme of things.

So, if you want to study something and learn a new skill over time, you don't have to dedicate hours and hours each day. Just dedicate a little bit of time every day, and that will take you far.

| Action Step |
| --- |
| Decide right now how much time per day you are going to dedicate to reading. Separate and break down the time by fun and learning (if you only plan to read for fun, then lucky you!) |
| Head over to http://debbiedrum.com/buzzreadvids, and share your goal in the comments sections. |
| Make a commitment to stick to your reading goal no matter what. |

# CHAPTER 18

# HOW TO TRACK YOUR
# READING PROGRESS

I CREATED A SIMPLE Google spreadsheet, wherein I paste all the books I read, and I measure how long it takes me to get through each book.

Some books take longer than others, as I may only be reading very few pages a day because it might be harder material to get through.

Some books, as you know, require more brain power. Some books—some fiction, for instance—require less brain power.

My spreadsheet looks like this:

| # | Purchase Date | Book | Time It Took To Complete | Pages |
|---|---|---|---|---|
| 5 | 3/26 | UNLIMITED MEMORY — How to Use Advanced Learning Strategies to Learn Faster, Remember More and be More Productive — GRANDMASTER KEVIN HORSLEY | 4/3 | 207 |
| 6 | 3/27 | HARRY POTTER and the SORCERER'S STONE — J.K. ROWLING | 4/2 (7 days) | 309 pgs |

I love my spreadsheet. It makes me happy, and it reminds me of all the hard work I am putting into achieving my goals. I highly recommend you track your progress, even if it's purely for bragging rights.

I have a spreadsheet template available for you for free at: **http://debbiedrum.com/buzzreadvids**

# CHAPTER 19

# WHAT SHOULD YOU READ FIRST?

THE EXCITING PART IS deciding what to read first. There are a bunch of places you can purchase books, rent books, and even get books for free.

First and foremost, you should read what you've always wanted to read, a book that will give you a lot of satisfaction. After that, you will naturally find related books that will interest you, probably with some help from Amazon, because they will recommend similar books in the same or related categories.

Here are four popular options on how to get books on your digital devices.

## 1. PURCHASE BOOKS ON AMAZON

Amazon.com is the biggest marketplace to find great books, old and new. You can easily get the books onto your reading device, and within minutes, you can have any book at your fingertips. It's a beautiful thing.

You can purchase books on Amazon.com; however, you can also get free books from a multitude of authors who are running promotions.

Visit   this   link   to   find   free   books   to   download:
**http://debbiedrum.com/top100free**

## 2. Join Kindle Unlimited ($9.99 per month)

Kindle Unlimited is a monthly program you can join on Amazon. You can find it here: **http://debbiedrum.com/kindleunlimited**
You pay a monthly fee of $9.99, but then you have free access to any book that is in the Kindle Unlimited Program. I recently signed up to Kindle Unlimited, and I am enjoying the program. If you read two or more books per month, the service pays for itself.

Note: You can only have ten books out at once with Kindle Unlimited.

## 3. Borrow eBooks From the Library (Without Leaving Home)

With Overdrive (**http://overdrive.com**) you can borrow free e-books, audiobooks, and more from your library's digital collection. All you need to get started is an internet connection and a library card.

Here are the steps to work with Overdrive:

### Step 1: Download the Overdrive App.

Simply go to the app store, search for the Overdrive app, and download it. It's free.

### Step 2: Find your library

With Overdrive's mobile app, you can use the library finder to find your library for easy access later. You will need your library card when setting up your account.

The app is free and available from most major app marketplaces, including Google Play and the Apple App Store.

You can also find your library by visiting overdrive.com, where you can search for titles and libraries in the Overdrive network.

## Step 3: Browse

Open your library's digital connection. There, you can explore titles on the homepage, browse Subjects or Collections, or search for a specific title or author.

After you open the collection or perform a search, you can use the filters to find exactly what you are looking for.

## Step 4: Borrow

You can borrow titles right from the homepage or from search results, or tap or click a title to go to its details page, where you can learn more before you borrow.

When prompted, sign in using your library card, a free Overdrive account, or a Facebook account.

If you use an Overdrive or a Facebook account, you will be prompted to save the valid library card to your account the first time you sign in.

## Step 5: Enjoy

All of your borrowed titles will appear on your Loans page on the mobile app. If you're using the Overdrive app, you can download borrowed eBooks and audiobooks to your app bookshelf, to easily access them on or offline.

If you're using a computer and have an internet connection, you can read, watch, or listen to most titles right in your browser.

You can also download eBooks and audiobooks to your hard drive and enjoy them offline, or transfer them to compatible e-readers or mp3 players.

## LEARN MORE

There are a lot of other things you can do with your library's digital collection, such as place books on hold, add titles to your wish list, and return titles early.

If you need assistance, visit Overdrive Help for Getting Started guides, How To articles, troubleshooting tips, and more at **http://overdrive.com**.

## 4. FREE BOOK RESOURCES

There are tons of free book resources online. You can start by doing a Google search. Type in "Free books," and you'll find a ton of great results. There are always authors giving out books, especially when they want a review. You can also find free books in the public domain. Classics like Jane Eyre, Hamlet, and Pride and Prejudice are all available free in the public domain. See a list of some public-domain books here: **http://debbiedrum.com/grclassics**

Here is another great resource to find books in the public domain: **http://debbiedrum.com/publicdomainbooks**

You can find books in all genres—even children's books—in the public domain. Sometimes, books will come in the PDF format, so be sure to take a look at how to use The BuzzRead Method with PDFs, and follow the instructions given earlier in this book.

There you have it. The above links should give you a great start at finding more books to read. Over time and after speaking with some friends, you will likely receive all kinds of recommendations regarding where to find books to read. You'll be a pro in no time, and you'll have an endless queue of books to read.

# CHAPTER 20

# ESSENTIAL TOOLS YOU NEED (THERE ARE NOT MANY)

YOU BASICALLY NEED THREE tools—one is mandatory, and two are optional but highly recommended.

Obviously, the first tool you absolutely need is a device you can use for reading eBooks.

You can use:

- Phone (Apple or Samsung)
- iPad
- e-Reader (Kindle Fire)
- Any other device you can download the Kindle app onto. Most tablets have the accessibility function. If you own a device that I did not discuss in this book, then simply go to **http://youtube.com**, and search for a video with the keywords "Text To Speech [name of your device]." You will find a slew of videos come up.

The first optional tool, but one that is highly recommended, is a set of headphones. You don't always need to use headphones, but if you are in a public place or if you are in a noisy room, then you will certainly want to use them.

You need to concentrate and focus with The BuzzRead Method, and headphones help block out distractions.

Finally, your second optional tool is to activate some kind of TTS on your desktop or laptop computer. I recommend using the free TTS on your device, but you can also use one of the recommended apps I mentioned earlier.

In addition to learning to read books faster, The BuzzRead Method offers several other life-changing benefits. We'll go over some of them in the next chapter.

# CHAPTER 21

# ADDITIONAL BENEFITS OF THE BUZZREAD METHOD

WITH THE BUZZREAD METHOD, you will be able to read more books, and that is amazing. It will give you the freedom of knowing you can read anything, and it won't take you a year and a day to get through one book...even if parts of the book are boring!

The BuzzRead Method will help you stay focused because it forces you to keep going.

With traditional reading, two things can happen.

1. Your mind can wander, and you will completely stop reading and begin thinking about other things.
2. Your mind can wander, but somehow you will still be reading. You will get through the page or pages and will not know what the heck you've just read! Since you haven't retained any of the information, you will have no choice but to read it over again.

Neither of the above instances are good. They are stopping you from gaining progress in your reading. Essentially, you are wasting precious time! Time you could spend getting your work done, so you could have more time to play or do other things.

The BuzzRead Method helps you to stay on track because it keeps your mind from wandering, and it helps you get past the hard, tedious parts of books. For some reason, when I come across patches of reading material that are clumped together in big paragraphs without many breaks or dialogue, that's where I tend to slow down. Those sections of books take me longer to get through. With The BuzzRead Method, I can get through those parts very quickly.

Another major benefit of this method is, remember, because you are following along with the words on the screen while the device is reading out loud, you are working and training your eye muscles. Although this might seem like a little thing, this work will pay off. After you've spent some time using The BuzzRead Method, you will find you're even reading faster the traditional way because you've trained your eyes to move fast across the words and the page. Even though the TTS technology exists, and it's not going anywhere, you don't want to have to rely on it all the time. You're not going to have the technology for everything—for instance, you won't have access to TTS when you are taking a test—but in so many other instances, The BuzzRead Method will take you far.

The technique of working your eye muscles back and forth is a proven method to help people read faster. It's a method Jim Kwik teaches in his speed-reading course, and it's a method taught in every speed-reading app. We are training our eyes to move from side to side, not only at a faster pace but also without tiring as quickly. This can be compared to working out on a treadmill. The first day, we my move slowly and get winded quickly. However, if you keep practicing and you keep at it, you will notice you will not get tired as quickly as you did on day one, and your skills will improve dramatically in a short time. It's all the same concept!

As with anything else, though, you need to keep at it. Just because you are developing and working your muscles, that doesn't mean you can just stop, and they will stay strong forever. If you do sit-ups and crunches for six months and then stop, do you think you'll keep that defined six-pack for the rest of your life, or do you think it will start to disappear because you've stopped working those muscles? It's the *same concept*. You must continue honing your skills and keep using your newly trained muscles, so they will stay strong. The good news is you will always have this method—or superhuman skill—and you shouldn't ever want to stop!

The bottom line is that you will be improving your reading skills overall. You will be able to read business books, finance books, long fiction books, and even economics books. Books make you smarter, and the more you read, the more you will know. You can be a great resource for information, and you can also demand a higher salary!

You can learn anything you've always wanted to learn! For example, I am going to start reading books on cryptocurrencies, like the bitcoin. I've been wanting to learn about that topic for a long time, but I never thought I'd be able to with all the other books I wanted to read. Now, this is a possibility!

One last major benefit before I let you go on your merry reading way...

# CHAPTER 22

# GAIN FREEDOM FROM READING

READING MAKES YOU A better writer—and speaker, for that matter. In this day and age, being a good writer can be a ticket to financial freedom. Writing books like this one, writing online content (blogs and scripts), and even writing for other people (ghostwriting) can provide great sources of income, both full-time and part-time.

The great part about being a writer is that you can make money from the comfort of your home or from anywhere in the world! This is exactly what I do. I wake up and create awesome content for myself and others...and I make a full-time income from this. While many people have to get up with an alarm clock, commute to work, and answer to a boss, I don't have to do any of that! It's a beautiful thing.

I've developed many systems and products to make money from home, but the single skill that got me here is my ability to write and create content. I am not the best writer in the world, and I haven't even taken many writing lessons, but I like to write and express myself through the written word. I find that I express myself better through writing, although practice and experience has helped me improve my public speaking technique over the years.

When I started The BuzzRead Method, I really wanted to help people like me—people who were slower readers and who often became frustrated when confronted with longer or more difficult books. That's why I wrote this book.

## THE MAGIC PROCESS

I've written a lot over the course of my career, but my process lately has been to read using The BuzzRead Method for about a half an hour and then immediately begin work on my current writing project. This works well for me because hearing how another successful writer writes and expresses points translates over to my own writing. I'm not actually saying what the other author is saying, but the mannerisms, teaching styles, and even the layout will come across in my writing, too. In essence, I am learning, practicing, and implementing from works of best-selling authors! I recommend you give this a try; it's a great way to hone your skills and become a better writer. Use The BuzzRead Method to read for thirty minutes or so, and then immediately do some writing afterward. Make a habit of doing this daily, because as with anything else you want to get better at, practice makes progress! I am not saying you will become the best writer in the world, and even great writers need editors, but you will definitely improve with practice.

# CHAPTER 23

# BEYOND THE BUZZ

AGAIN, WHILE THE BUZZREAD Method will help you speed through books, you might want some additional help reading faster without the assistance of TTS.

Gaining speed-reading skills means improving your focus, enhancing your level of understanding and comprehension, boosting your memory, and most importantly, freeing up a tremendous amount of time that you can use to positively develop your life in other ways.

Studies show that the average adult reads approximately two hundred words per minute. In contrast, the average college student reads at a rate of approximately three hundred and twenty-five words per minute. That one hundred twenty-five extra words read each minute can be seriously life changing for anyone who wants to lead a more productive life.

What if I told you that almost everyone, including you, has the potential to learn how to read at speeds of up to five hundred words per minute?

The key is learning how to speed read effectively and practicing your skills on a regular basis, both of which are very possible if you use any one or a combination of the following techniques.

## IMPROVING YOUR FOCUS AND CONCENTRATION

Learning how to read faster requires you to develop a keen ability to focus and concentrate on the text in front of you. By learning to ignore or block out everything other than your reading material, you automatically enhance your ability to read faster.

## HAND PACING

An effective technique for learning how to read faster is known as hand pacing. All it requires is using a finger, pen, or other pointing device to move across the page directly below the line of text you're reading. This helps to improve your reading speed by allowing you to set your own ever-increasing pace.

## WORD GROUPING

While highly effective, word grouping is one of the more challenging speed-reading techniques to grasp. It involves reading and processing words as groups, instead of trying to read them individually, which reduces overall reading speed dramatically.

## MINIMIZING SUB-VOCALIZATION

We have talked about sub-vocalization a lot so far. Sub-vocalization is reading out loud inside your head, and it's a real killer when it comes to learning how to read faster.

Vocalizing or speaking words as you read slows your reading speed down dramatically. That's because it reduces your mind reading speed to the same levels as your speaking speed, which tends to be a lot slower. By eliminating a tendency to sub-vocalize, you gradually improve your ability to read faster.

## SCANNING AND PREVIEWING

Two other techniques that help to improve your reading speed are known as scanning and previewing.

These methods help to enhance your comprehension of a subject by skimming over the text to identify relevant information, such as names, numbers, and trigger words in areas like subheadings, lists, and graphs.

By scanning and previewing a page, you quickly grasp the major idea behind the piece of text, which improves your overall reading speed and cuts down on the amount of time necessary for comprehension.

## PRACTICE READING FASTER

Simply making a consistent and regular effort to read words on a page at a faster pace than you usually do dramatically increases your reading speed over time. Set aside a small block of time each day to practice your speed-reading techniques, and you will quickly reap the benefits.

## WORK WITH A SPEED-READING INSTRUCTOR

One of the best methods of boosting your ability to read faster is to work with a professional speed-reading instructor. They can help you to identify and take advantage of your primary learning style and help you to reverse and eliminate any bad reading habits that can keep you from your reading goals.

This lets you enhance your speed-reading skills quickly, while also allowing you to boost your productivity, memory, and comprehension levels.

## FINALLY, READ MORE BOOKS

Now that you will be able to read books faster and better with The BuzzRead Method, you will have a huge advantage because you'll be able to learn faster. You can buzz through speed-reading books, and grasp the main ideas and strategies, even without reading the entire book. I highly recommend joining the Kindle Unlimited program because there are tons of great books—including books on the topic of speed-reading—on the Kindle Unlimited program.

Pick up strategies that will work with your learning style and use them. Repetition and practice will be your best friend.

# CHAPTER 24

# WRAP UP

I HOPE YOU ENJOYED learning The BuzzRead Method and everything that goes along with it. I did my very best to clearly outline and share with you all my secrets. I have achieved a great deal of success using this method. Just yesterday, I needed to learn something quickly, and I downloaded a two hundred-page book and finished reading it in two days. Before I began using The BuzzRead Method, I would not have even attempted such a feat. But here I am, reading more than I ever thought I could, and I can't wait for you to do the same.

Remember, there aren't too many rules to follow, but you need to at least do the basics.

1. **Read with Purpose**—don't just speed through the book and expect the content to stick in your brain. You need to be deliberate with your practice. Dedicating a small amount of time per day (thirty to forty minutes of intense focus) will put you on track to retaining what you are reading. You can work up to doing more reading once you get used to the process.

2. **Follow Along**—The BuzzRead Method is not just about passively listening while you walk your dog, do the dishes, or lift weights. You need to be actively engaged in the content, and that means following along with the text as Siri reads to you. You will notice a

huge difference in your reading speed when you read without the TTS after just about a week of practice.

3. **Create and Commit to a Routine**—You need to make reading books part of your daily life. Even if you read for just thirty minutes a day, that's a great start! You will find you begin to enjoy your reading time, and you may even find it a bit relaxing! Here's another great tip: Use time you might otherwise spend sitting idle to do your reading. For example, if you have to wait in the doctor's office or wait in the car while your significant other runs into the supermarket for food, you should always have your device with you, so you can do your daily reading. It's a great way to use your time more effectively!

4. **Slow is Fast**—This is a term my high school math teacher would use, and I will never forget it. She used the phrase in reference to math because when you do a math problem too quickly, you tend to make silly mistakes, but if you do it slowly, you will save time because you won't make those mistakes. The same is true for almost anything in life. As I suggested earlier, you can read multiple books. You might have a really hard book that is packed with information that you might have to move through slowly. However, you can couple that reading with a fiction book that doesn't require too much brain power. Some books might take two or three weeks to get through, but you'll definitely get through them with The BuzzRead Method. Not every book has to be read at lightning speed!

5. **Have Fun, and Put Your New Knowledge to Good Use**—Don't put too much pressure on yourself just because you developed a new superpower. Also, pay it forward, and share your new knowledge with a friend; they'll love you for it!

# ADDITIONAL HELP
## AND RESOURCES

I WANTED TO PROVIDE you with some additional training in case you want to see more of a hands-on approach to The BuzzRead Method. This is my gift to you for purchasing this book! All you need to do is head over to **http://debbiedrum.com/buzzreadvids** and you will have access to:

- Over-the-shoulder training videos
- Templates for measuring your progress
- Ask me questions inside – there's a dedicated comments section where I will get notified of your questions
- And more…

Simply register your account—it's free to sign up—and you will get access to the members' area immediately. You will also be able to ask me any questions you have! I look forward to seeing you there!

**Note:** I couldn't cover the setup of every device in this book. If you have a specific device you need help setting up, please ask me in the members' area, and I will do my best to help you.

# ABOUT THE AUTHOR

DEBBIE DRUM IS A bestselling author, product creator, software developer, a loving wife and mom of two furry pals.

Since 2010, Debbie has been helping authors and product creators market and become authorities in their specific niches. She uses the power of video marketing and simple, straight-to-the-point content to get that done.

When Debbie's not writing and filming videos, she is active playing sports, exercising, and probably learning some kind of new skill, such as playing the drums and saxophone.

Debbie's formula for success in life is her mix of a go-getter attitude coupled with tremendous heart and determination, which she applies to everything she does. She believes superpowers are made and not born. Put your mind to something, and you will achieve success. It's really that simple.

## CONNECT WITH DEBBIE DRUM

Please connect with me! You can find me hanging out on the following social media channels:

Facebook: **https://www.facebook.com/debbiedrummarketing**

YouTube: **https://www.youtube.com/user/deborahdrum**

Twitter: **https://twitter.com/DebDrum05**

Website: **http://debbiedrum.com**

# THANK YOU...
# AND ONE TINY FAVOR, PLEASE

Thank you for reading my book!

I really value your feedback and would love to hear what you have to say.

I need your input to make the next version better.

**Please leave me a helpful review on Amazon by going to this link:**
http://debbiedrum.com/readbetterfasterreview

It would really help, and I value your opinion!

# GET BOOK DISCOUNTS AND DEALS

Get discounts and special deals on our bestselling books at
**www.tckpublishing.com/bookdeals**

82722132R00074

Made in the USA
Columbia, SC
05 December 2017